Entering the Covenant

Entering

Compiled by
Mandell I. Ganchrow, M.D.

Edited by
Mrs. Ethel Gottlieb

Published by the

the Covenant

להכניסו בבריתו
של אברהם אבינו

An Anthology of Divrei Torah for
Bris Milah and Pidyon Haben

TO OUR CHILDREN

Joshua, Harrison, and Logan

ברוך צבי, ישראל יעקב, ורפאל חנניה

❧ ❧ ❧

זאת בריתי אשר תשמרו ביני וביניכם ובין זרעך אחריך

*This is My covenant which you shall keep
between Me and you and your descendants after you.*
(Bereishis 17:10)

❧ ❧ ❧

WE DEDICATE THIS BOOK TO YOU,
OUR GREATEST TREASURE.
MAY THE IDEALS, BELIEFS, TRADITIONS AND VALUES
WHICH ARE ROOTED IN OUR COVENANT WITH HASHEM
BE REFLECTED IN YOUR ACTIONS AND
TRANSMITTED FROM GENERATION TO GENERATION.

Lauren and Martin Geller
מרדכי יעקב ועליזה

❧ Table of Contents

Vayikra

Bamidbar

Devarim

Yamim Tovim

Insightful Essays

➳ Preface

HE MISHNAH IN *NEDARIAM* (31B) CLEARLY ELUCIDATES THE IMPORTANCE
and centrality of the *Mitzvah* of *Bris Milah* (circumcision) in the Jewish
life cycle.

Among its attributes is a connection to the covenant between Avraham
and G-d. It is, says Rabbi Yose, such a great event that it even overrides the
strict laws of Shabbos. The Holy One would not have created the world,
notes the Mishnah, had it not been for the *Mitzvah* of *Bris Milah*. The
Gemora (32a) adds that circumcision is such a great *Mitzvah* that it is equal
to all of the other commandments of the Torah.

The act of circumcision originated with our father Abraham, at the age
of ninety-nine. He, subsequently, circumcised his son Ishmael, his household, and his son Isaac. The commandment of *Bris Milah*, which this volume celebrates, is integrally bound up with the covenant to inherit the
land of Israel. The failure to keep this commandment is punished by *kares*,
which in effect means the individual is ostracized or cut-off from the Jewish entity or polity.

The success of my anthology of *Divrei Torah — Sason VeSimcha* for the
occasion of *Sheva Brachos* encouraged me to undertake this project. It has
been a totally delightful experience to be stopped by total strangers rang-
ing from *Chassidim* to non-Orthodox and informed that they had just
utilized a *devar Torah* from our book at a recent *simcha*. Once again I am
gratified that all profits are being donated to a *kiruv* program of the Orthodox Union.

Having served as President of the Orthodox Union for six years and now
as Chairman of the Board, I note with great satisfaction the growth of
NCSY, especially our summer programs. Today, 40,000 young men and
women of high school age throughout the United States, Canada, Israel,
and Kharkov (Ukraine) benefit from NCSY.

The Orthodox community in the United States has made remarkable
strides in the last fifty years. The Torah community has never had a

"clergy" in the usual sense of the word. We have teachers and *rabbeim*. What is beautiful is that throughout the world the teaching of Torah, just like the learning of Torah, is not restricted to those with a formal degree of ordination. The most enjoyable part of my week, for almost ten years, has been the weekly Talmud class that I teach to former medical colleagues at Good Samaritan Hospital, a Catholic institution in Suffern, New York.

It is in that spirit that I express my appreciation to the dozens of contributors to this volume. The chapters are arranged according to the weekly *parshah*, as well as all the Jewish Festivals. Our contributors range from Torah scholars at the highest level to *baalabatim* in business, law, and medicine whose insight I pray will bring light to the subject.

Parents, grandparents, and others who must speak words of Torah at a *Shalom Zachor, Bris Milah* or *Pidyon Haben* should find the task much easier by utilizing the chapters of our book. In addition to an overview of the *Halachos* of *Bris Milah* there are some general chapters on *Bris Milah,* a name's significance and *Pidyon Haben*. I have also included a chapter by Rabbi Ephraim Sturm on *"Upsharing"* and Wimple. Two friends, Debbie Schwartz and Liz Muschel, have written about *Bris Milah* from a mother's point of view.

I am indebted to my most competent and dedicated editor, Ethel Gottlieb whose professionalism, zeal and knowledge have made my part very easy. Without her direction and sense of priorities there could not have been a book. Her experience as an editor has allowed the material to flow in a beautiful and easy to comprehend manner. My secretary, Frances Breiner, was diligent, not only in acting as the liaison with Ethel but in helping me to secure the responses of the contributors. Her computer skills were invaluable. I thank Yehuda Gordon, from the Orthodox Union, who skillfully typed all the Hebrew entries of the book.

I also wish to thank Rabbi Raphael B. Butler, former Executive Vice-President, and Sheldon Fliegelman, our Director of Development, for their encouragement, as well as Rabbi Moshe Krupka, Director of Synagogue and Community Services for acting as liaison with ArtScroll Publications.

It has been six years since the publication of our anthology *Sason VeSimcha* and my devotion and debt to Sheila, my wife of 39 years, has only grown. The encouragement of my mother, Kate Ganchrow, who at almost

90 is the matriarch of our family, my children, Malkie and Paul, Banji and Ari, and Brina and Elli, as well as our six grandchildren, Zachary, Jake, Carlie, Jack, Jonah, and Matthew have given me the spirit and strength to devote my energies to the needs of the *Klal*.

May this volume, with its pearls of Torah wisdom, help many to enjoy the gift of life that the Almighty has granted to someone close to them as they celebrate the *Bris Milah* of a child, grandchild or loved one.

Mandell I. Ganchrow, MD
Monsey, New York
June 5, 2001 / 15 Sivan 5761

Overview of Halachos

_____ *Rabbi Aaron J. Fink, Certified Mohel*

MAZEL TOV! IT'S A BOY. WITH THESE JOYFUL WORDS EXCITEMENT AND AWE pulsate through the new father's soul, reconfirming our trust in G-d and the miracle of life. Whether the baby is a first-born or a new addition, welcome to fatherhood and enjoy your son!

After the initial jubilation, thoughts immediately turn to the opportunity to fulfill one of Judaism's defining *Mitzvos* — להכניסו בבריתו של אברהם אבינו — "to enter him into the covenant of Abraham," in short his *Bris.*

The *Bris,* frequently described as ritual circumcision, is anything but mere ritual. Rather, it defines the character of the Jewish nation. It is the essence of the eternal bond between Hashem and His people. We brand ourselves as Jews by learning from the most tender age our responsibility to reveal inner truth. The Talmud recounts how the Roman emperor Turnus Rufus, challenged Rabbi Akiva, "What is greater, the accomplishments of man or of G-d?" Rabbi Akiva responded, "Man's accomplishments are superior." The emperor mocked Rabbi Akiva and pointed to the beauty of nature, the magnificent sky above the horizon and said, "Can man do this?" Whereupon Rabbi Akiva responded with sheaves of wheat alongside loaves of bread and retorted, "Who made the bread — is it not the power of human creativity?" Such is the analogy to *Bris Milah.*

Man is created in the image of Hashem, but it is up to each individual to perfect himself. We are born with so much opportunity and unbelievable

_____
Rabbi Aaron Fink is a resident of Monsey, NY and is the Dean of Ateres Bais Yaakov. He is a practicing Mohel in Rockland County, New York.

potential, yet it is up to us to actualize it. This, Rabbi Akiva explained, is the message of *Bris Milah*. We are born imperfect. Just as the foreskin is to be removed to reveal the anatomy as G-d intended, we must improve ourselves to serve Hashem as He intends. With blood, sweat and tears we can do what it takes to make a difference, to serve as a light to all nations and reveal the hidden truths of G-d's glory for all to see. This was the mission of our patriarch Abraham who taught monotheism to a pagan world. It was he who was commanded to perform the first *Bris*. Yes, *Bris Milah* reminds us and teaches the newborn that we are put on this earth to make a difference through Torah, *Avodah* and *Maassim Tovim*. And so we bless the newborn, "As you have been introduced into your *Bris* so may you be initiated to strive for perfection in the study of Torah, a marriage of blessing and a life of good deeds." This lesson of self-improvement also sets the tone for creating a home and family environment by which to rear children into adulthood. Let us try to make each day better than the last. It is a sacred mission and challenge.

The Halachos and Minhagim — Rituals and Customs

THE *HALACHOS* AND *MINHAGIM* OF *BRIS MILAH* ARE DESCRIBED IN DETAIL IN THE *Shulchan Aruch*, the Code of Jewish Law. This overview is by no means exhaustive. Custom and ritual often reflect family *Minhag* and tradition. Where possible your local Rabbi or a regional *Mohel* should be consulted.

The *Mitzvah* of *Bris Milah* is serious; its neglect carries capital consequences. Preparations for this great event should begin as soon as possible after birth.

The first responsibility in preparing for your son's *Bris* is the selection of a competent and professional *Mohel*. Your son's *Mohel* should be a G-d fearing, Torah observant Jew who has earned a reputation for his performance and skill. When talking to a prospective *Mohel*, be sure to ask him if he will visit with you prior to the *Bris* to examine the baby and acquaint you with the details of the ceremony and procedure. Be sure to prepare a list of questions to ask him at that time. Your *Mohel* can help you set the date and time for the *Bris*, select an appropriate Hebrew name for your son, answer myriad questions about circumcision and discuss concepts of Judaism about which you are curious. Your *Mohel* should also be able to reassure you of his personal attention to post-*Bris* care, including a home visit if necessary to change or remove the dressing.

The customs surrounding the arrival a newborn son include: The *Shalom Zachor, Vacht Nacht, Bris,* and *Pidyon Haben* where applicable. We will discuss each one.

◆§ *Shalom Zachor:* The celebration of your new son's arrival begins the first Shabbos eve of his life. That Friday night is the traditional *Shalom Zachor* — welcome, newborn son. A variety of commentaries explain the significance of the celebration that follows the usual Sabbath meal and traditionally features the round garbanzo bean (*Arbis*) as well as pastries, candy and beer. They explain that the newborn senses the arrival of Shabbos, which, is also described as a covenant (*bris*). He feels ashamed that he has not yet entered into the covenant himself and so we gather together to cheer him up and remind him that his own entry into the covenant is just around the corner.

◆§ *Vacht Nacht:* The evening before the *Bris* is another opportunity to anticipate the morrow's ceremony with what is called in Yiddish, *Vacht Nacht.* This gathering features children who come to the newborn's house to recite the *Shema Yisrael* prayer and the blessing of *Ha'malach Hagoel* in unison, alongside the newborn. It is a solemn moment when we offer our prayers to Hashem that the *Bris* itself should be a safe and uncomplicated procedure.

◆§ *Bris Milah:* The **Bris** should take place on the eighth day, even if it is Shabbos or Yom Kippur, provided the baby is in good health. (Exceptions are listed below.) A *Bris* may *not* take place at night (after sundown). Day 8 is calculated by counting from the day of birth which is considered day 1. The Jewish calendar begins its day at nightfall. This is important in calculating the appropriate *Bris* date when a baby is born at night. For example, a baby born Tuesday morning would have his *Bris* the following Tuesday. However, a baby born Tuesday evening after sunset would have his *Bris* the following Wednesday. Technically speaking, birth is determined from the time the baby's head is fully delivered. If your son's birth was close to sundown the timing of his head's emergence from the birth canal could effect the day of his *Bris.* Baby's born during the twilight period between sundown and starlight are considered to be born on the following day.

⇦§ A **Shabbos Bris** occurs when a number of conditions are met:
- A baby is born between *starlight* Friday evening and *sunset* Saturday night.
- The baby is born naturally — a caesarean-section delivery **eliminates** the possibility of a Shabbos *Bris*.
- The baby is healthy.
- It is the eighth day.

A baby born during twilight Friday evening (after sunset but before starlight) would have his *Bris* on Sunday.

⇦§ A **Delayed Bris** may be required should health concerns, both *Halachic* and medical, be identified. The most common heath precaution is physiological jaundice. A bilirubinotomy, performed by your physician can determine the jaundice level. Your *Mohel* will advise you on the count that precludes a timely *Bris*. Infection is a more serious concern. Infection, even conjunctivitis, can postpone a *Bris* as late as the morning of the scheduled circumcision. A baby treated with antibiotics, even prophylactically, will need to wait at least seven 24 hour periods from the time his doctor has concluded he is in tip top shape to schedule his *Bris*. You should keep your *Mohel* informed of your son's medical status. He may want to contact your physician to discuss your baby's medical condition.

The ceremony that accompanies the *Bris* is rich in heritage and tradition. The typical ceremony contains the following steps in which you can invite your relatives and/or friends to participate. They are presented in sequence.

⇦§ *Kvatter / Kvatterein:* a couple or series of family, relatives and friends who usher the baby into his *Bris*. This honor is considered a good omen for those who are not yet blessed with children, or not yet blessed with a son to enjoy a *Simcha* of their own. While the *Kvatter* couple(s) carry the baby into the room where the *Bris* is to be performed the *Mohel* welcomes the baby and recites a special selection of verses which refer to the Prophet Eliyahu and his covenant with G-d.

⇦§ *Kisay Shel Eliyahu:* Our Rabbis teach us that Eliyahu *HaNavi*, Elijah the Prophet attends every *Bris* service. For this reason Eliyahu is known in the liturgy as the *Malach HaBris,* the Angel of the *Bris*. A chair is designated for him at the ceremony and it is a prestigious honor to place the baby on "Eliyahu's lap for a blessing." As the designated individual places the baby on the *Kisay Shel Eliyahu* the *Mohel* recites a prayer asking for Eliyahu *HaNavi* to stand at his side and assist him in performing the delicate procedure.

◦§ *Me'al Hakisay:* An individual is recognized with the honor of lifting the infant from Eliyahu *HaNavi*'s lap. The infant is then placed in the arms of his father in anticipation of the *Bris.*

◦§ *Sandek:* The *Sandek,* is the individual who will actually hold the baby during the *Bris.* He does not have to watch the procedure. He should follow the guidance of the *Mohel* as how to firmly but lovingly hold the baby during the *Bris.* The *Sandek* is often a grandparent, Rabbi or spiritual mentor. The Sages tell us that the *Sandek* has the ability to imbue spiritual and character traits into the youngster. Some families have the custom of not using the same *Sandek* more than once per family. For those with this custom, siblings would not have the same *Sandek,* though cousins could. The honor of *Sandek* is quite prestigious. In fact, the joy of an individual who knows that he is to be a *Sandek* at a *Bris* exempts the entire congregation from certain prayers of contrition (*Tachanun*) in the daily service that day.

At this point in time the actual *Bris* is performed. The *Mohel* will recite a *Berachah* and perform the circumcision. Immediately following the *Mohel*'s *Berachah,* the father will recite the Father's Blessing thanking G-d for granting him the opportunity to enter his son into the covenant of Abraham:

ברוך אתה ה' אלקינו מלך העולם אשר קדשנו
במצותיו וצונו להכניסו בבריתו של אברהם אבינו

◦§ *Amida L'Brachos:* When the procedure is complete, an individual so honored will be called upon to hold the baby for a special *berachah* which begins with Kiddush on wine, followed by a blessing beseeching G-d to protect and guide this child in the merit of the Covenant now permanently marked upon him.

◦§ *Mevareich:* A cup of wine is poured and the *Mevareich* recites the Kiddush and *Berachah* noted above.

◦§ *Amidah L' Krias Shem:* Having been circumcised the "guest of honor" is now ready to receive his Jewish name. An individual will be honored with holding the baby for the naming service.

◦§ *Krias Shem:* The Rabbi, *Mohel* or prominent guest performs the naming ceremony. After the baby is named the "*Kvatter* couple" return to complete the "round trip" and carry the baby back to his mother. The *Mohel* will usually want to check the baby before he is nursed or fed. The *Aleinu* prayer is then recited followed by wishes of Mazel Tov and a festive meal (*Seudas Bris*).

☙ The **Seudas Bris,** the festive meal is an important part of the *Bris* celebration. The commentaries point out that the biblical text informs us (homiletically) that our father Abraham sponsored a banquet celebrating the *Bris* of the patriarch Isaac (*Parsha Vayeira; Bereishis* 21:8).

At the conclusion of the meal a special introduction is added to the Grace after Meals. A series of *Harachaman* blessings are inserted into the concluding portion of the Grace after Meals liturgy. These six requests of the Al-mighty may be assigned for recitation to honor different individuals. Though a traditional cup of wine is held during the introductory portion of the After Meal Service it is not passed around during the *Harachamans.*

☙ *Pidyon Haben:* A first-born baby boy born of a natural delivery may require a *Pidyon Haben,* a Redemption of the First Born ceremony when he is 30 days old. A *Pidyon Haben* is a rare celebration. Only first-born babies meeting the following criteria are eligible for the service.

The baby must be:
– Naturally born.
– Born of a mother who had no prior pregnancies or miscarriages.
– Born of a father or mother who is not himself or herself the offspring of a father who is a *Kohen* or a *Levi*.

Consult your Rabbi or *Mohel* to assist you in determining your child's status for a *Pidyon Haben.*

With the *Bris* concluded, the responsibilities of parenthood are now upon you. It is the work of a lifetime. Our children are our truest legacy. They will carry the lessons of our life into the future. Your son is now ready to embark on the road to become a proud Jew worthy of the distinction of the Children of Israel. May the traditions of our heritage continue to inspire you. May the commitment to self-improvement guide you and may your love for family and G-d deliver you much *Nachas* and joy for 120 healthy and happy years.

Sefer Bereishis

פרשת בראשית
Parshas Bereishis

_____ *Rabbi Dr. Moshe Tendler*

כשם שנכנס לברית כן יכנס לתורה ולחופה ולמעשים טובים — "Just as he en-tered the Covenant so may he enter into the Torah, the marriage canopy and good deeds." This blessing is bestowed upon the happy parents of a son who has just been inducted into the Covenant of Abraham. It is more than an expression of good wishes by those assembled for the future development of the child. The word כשם, "just as," adds an ancillary bless-ing — the blessing of the proper balance between nature and nurture during the formative years of this child.

The first *Sidrah* of our Torah records the tragic, horrifying fratricide committed by Cain. The Creator of Heaven and Earth, all contained therein, and of man and woman, demands of Cain, "Where is your brother?" Cain's response would seem to be the epitome of *chutzpah* and disrespect toward the G-d he knows so well. "Am I my brother's keeper?" evades the piercing question of Hashem. Cain knew very well that it meant "Why did you kill your brother?" Indeed, we must question why Hashem ordered Cain's response to be included in the sanctified text of our Torah. So brazen a response would seem not to deserve to be eternalized in our Torah text.

Its inclusion in the *Sidrah* compels us to search for deeper meaning in Cain's irreverent retort. I suggest that it was a brilliant rebuttal of Hashem's accusation. "Am *I* my brother's keeper? *You,* Hashem bear the

_____

Rabbi Tendler is rav of Community Synagogue of Monsey, New York and Rosh Yeshiva of the Rabbi Isaac Elchanan Theological Seminary in New York City.

responsibility. You gave me the nature, the genetic predisposition to be a murderer. It was within Your power to fashion mankind without the ability to murder members of their own species. Most infrahuman species were so fashioned by Your Hand!"

Cain's retort is recorded to reject Cain's genetic defense. No one is coerced by his genome to violate Hashem's laws for mankind. Indeed, people have different personalities and varying dispositions that expose them to temptation and to sin. Hashem had previously instructed Cain when he displayed anger and disappointment at the refusal of Hashem to accept his less than gracious sacrifice: " . . . the sin lies at the threshold and it is attractive to you, but I gave you the ability to master your desire to sin" (*Bereishis* 4:7).

How this new son of our people will balance the tensions between his genetic predispositions, the secular cultural forces he will confront during maturation, and the imperatives of a Torah life-style, will determine his success as a Jew and a *ben Torah.* Therefore, all assembled extend their blessing to his parents: כשם — just as today he has participated in the great *mitzvah* of *Milah* without the impact of the negative forces of a secular culture, so too, when he matures to a life of Torah and *Mitzvos,* the education he will receive from his parents will give him full mastery, והוא ימשול, over all the negative influences, as he achieves his goal to live a life that finds favor בעיני אלקים ואדם — in the eyes of G-d and Man.

פרשת נח
Parshas Noach

Dr. William Schwartz

THE FIRST TIME THE WORD *BRIS* OCCURS IN *TANACH* IS IN *PARSHAS NOACH:* והקמתי את בריתי . . . ויאמר אלקים זאת אות הברית אשר אני נתן ביני וביניכם . . . — "And I will את קשתי נתתי בענן והיתה לאות ברית . . . וזכרתי את בריתי confirm My convenant (see 6:18) . . . And G-d said, "This is the sign of the covenant that I have given between Me and you . . . I have set My rainbow in the cloud and it shall be a sign of the covenant . . . I will remember My convenant" (*Bereishis* 9:11-15). Hashem refers to this as a ברית עולם, "everlasting covenant" (9:16). The rainbow that Hashem created to show mankind that He will never again destroy the world with water, represents a one-way promise from G-d to man. It requires no new commitment on man's part, no promise to accept any new rules, no obligation to avoid the חמס (robbery [6:11]) that brought about the Flood. It is a physical sign that G-d created to demonstrate His good faith. The *bris* of *Milah,* on the other hand, demonstrates our acceptance of Hashem's rules. It, too, seems to be a one-way sign, this time on the part of the Jew, to accept Hashem's laws and to create a visible sign of that dedication. Just as the physical act of circumcision represents our being a partner with Hashem in creation, and the completion of the male body, it also demonstrates the fulfillment of the complete cycle in the relationship between G-d and man. For the Jew, the *Milah* symbolizes our willingness and commitment to accept G-d and our being an *Am Segulah.* It is a physical sign that manifests our eternal devotion to G-d, just as the rainbow symbolizes His dedication to mankind.

Dr. Schwartz, is an ophthalmologist practicing in Rockland County, New York.

Bris Milah really is a two-way covenant. We *perform* the *Milah,* but G-d uses it to demonstrate His continuing relationship to the Jew.

Concerning *Bris Milah,* the *pasuk* says: . . . והקמתי את בריתי ביני ובינך לדרתם לברית עולם — "I will ratify My convenant, between Me and you . . . throughout their generations as an everlasting Convenant" (*Bereishis* 17:7).

And concerning the rainbow, it says: והיתה לאות ברית ביני ובין הארץ — "it shall be a sign of the covenant between Me and the earth" (ibid. 9:13).

Both symbols are an אות, a symbolic representation of an eternal covenant.

The *Maharal* refers to *Bris Milah* as being למעלה מן הטבע, supernatural. The reason is that Hashem created the world in seven days, but the act of *Bris Milah* does not take place until the eighth day. Seven days mark the completion of the natural order, the eighth day is one day beyond the natural creation. The *Mabul* (Flood) is also למעלה מן הטבע. A flood is a natural event, but G-d promised that He will never again bring a flood to destroy mankind. G-d, therefore, took the *Mabul* out of the realm of *tevah,* of natural events. He declared the *Mabul* to be a supernatural phenomenon. By performing a *bris* on the eighth day, the Jew shows that he is willing to live למעלה מן הטבע. He is in effect saying that just as G-d has promised mankind not to destroy it, the Jew promises G-d to place this אות upon his body as an eternal sign of dedication to Him. *Bris Milah* demonstrates that man can perfect himself and achieve a higher level than the "natural" way he was created. For this reason, explains the *Maharal,* the Jew accepts a commitment to live a life in a manner that is למעלה מן הטבע — he is prepared to try and perfect himself to develop a closer relationship to G-d which transcends his natural place in creation.

May the parents of the רך הנמול merit to raise him to fulfill the mission of all Jews throughout the centuries — to dedicate himself to Torah and *Mitzvos,* as perfectly as possible. Our hope and prayer is that he should be a source of great joy and pride to his family and *Klal Yisrael.*

פרשת לך לך
Parshas Lech Lecha

_____ Rabbi Pinchas Stolper_

THE MIDRASH (*BEREISHIS RABBAH*) TEACHES THAT WHEN G-D COMMANDED Avraham to circumcise himself, Avraham first consulted with his three friends, Onair, Ner and Mamrei. The commentators are astounded. Avraham underwent ten trials imposed upon him by G-d, some — such as the command to sacrifice Yitzchak, or being cast into the fiery oven, which Avraham survived — were far more traumatic and dangerous than circumcision. Why would Avraham consult his friends concerning this specific "trial?"

Our Rabbis teach (*Sotah* 47), "It is a principle that the left hand pushes away while the right hand brings close." The sublime quality of Avraham was that his "right hand" brought many people closer. His dominant quality was *chessed,* love and kindness. His door was always open to wayfarers. He was the exemplar, the master, of love, kindness, caring and concern. His entire life was devoted to influencing and inspiring strangers to acknowledge, love, and worship Hashem.

Avraham understood that the commandment of circumcision demonstrates the removal of that spiritually undesirable part of the body and symbolizes removing the "barrier" which impedes man's spiritual development. The purpose of *Milah* is to remove, to push away. Avraham feared that if he would now become known as a fighter in the battle against evil, rather than in the creation of good, he would weaken his power to attract and bring closer. Avraham, therefore, solved this problem by consulting his three friends who collectively represented the nations of the world.

_____

Rabbi Stolper is former senior executive of the Orthodox Union.

When Onair, Ner and Mamrei agreed that circumcision would not cause disunity or widen the chasm between Avraham and the world, that Avraham would continue to be known as the force for "the right hand drawing closer" he felt comforted and proceeded to circumcise his son.

It is our prayer that by excising that part of the body which symbolizes lack of restraint the newborn will join the People of Avraham and draw closer to the worship of Hashem.

Why Does Milah Require Two Blessings?

A final thought: It is generally our practice to pronounce one blessing on a *mitzvah*. Circumcision, however, is unique in that in addition to the first blessing, "To circumcise" we also recite a second blessing, "Who commanded us to initiate the infant into the Covenant of our Father Avraham." This second blessing teaches us that circumcision is not only a *mitzvah* which we are commanded to perform, circumcision also demands that every Jew identify with the covenant of Avraham and be included in it. In other words, the *Bris Milah,* the Covenant of *chessed* of our Father Avraham, obligates each and every Jew to become a practitioner of Avraham's quality of *chessed.*

Chessed is Avraham's specific and overriding character trait. It was Avraham's insight that creation itself was an act of *chessed.* This insight gave Avraham the perseverance to recognize the need to emulate his Creator. It was with *chessed* that Avraham founded the Jewish people. As a result G-d rewarded Avraham with the Covenant of *Bris Milah,* the covenant of *chessed.*

Through the covenant of *Bris Milah,* the quality of *chessed* is embedded in our very being. *Chessed* is sealed in the organ which makes it possible for a man and a woman to join together in creating children, mankind's greatest challenge and accomplishment. Through our expression of love for and knowledge of another person we become partners with G-d in creation. The covenant of *Bris Milah* was G-d's great gift to Avraham and, through him to all of us. It allows us not only to emulate G-d but to join with G-d in continually recreating and perfecting His world.

Through *Milah* we identify with G-d's path-of-*chessed* and identify with Avraham concerning whom G-d said: "For I have known Avraham in order that he be able to command his descendants to follow My path by acting with righteousness and justice" (*Bereishis* 18:19).

פרשת וירא
Parshas Vayeira

_____ *Rabbi Rafael G. Grossman*

"*A*ND IT CAME TO PASS AFTER THESE WORDS, THAT G-D DID TEST *A*BRAHAM" *(Bereishis 22:1). What is meant by 'after,' R. Johanan said on the authority of R. Jose b. Zimra: 'After' the words of Satan ,as it is written, 'And the child grew, and was weaned; and Abraham made a great feast the same day that Isaac was weaned.' Thereupon Satan said to the Almighty: 'Sovereign of the Universe! To this old man You did graciously grant the fruit of the womb at the age of one hundred, yet of all that banquet which he prepared, he did not have one turtledove or pigeon to sacrifice before You! Has he done anything that was but in honor of his son?' Replied He, 'Yet were I to say to him, "Sacrifice your son before Me," he would do so without hesitation.' Straightaway, 'God did test Abraham . . . And He said, 'Take, please your son.'* (Sanhedrin 89b)

Satan argued with G-d against His designation of Yitzchak as Avraham's heir. He contended that Avraham was himself deficient in faith, for he had not taught his son to actualize his knowledge and Yitzchak would therefore be unable to defend his beliefs. Yishmael, Avraham's other son by the concubine Hagar, demanded that his father's mantle be placed upon him. He, Yishmael, knew the skills of war and the duplicitous art of diplomacy. Therefore, he felt that he was more deserving of the inheritance to be the father of a great nation.

G-d's response was the testing of Avraham and the binding of Yitzchak (*Akeidah*). G-d demonstrated to them and to all future generations

_____

Rabbi Grossman is the Senior Rabbi of Baron Hirsch Synagogue in Memphis, Tennessee, and a past president of the Rabbinical Council of America.

what the strength of their faith could achieve.

Avraham's descendants have repeatedly been called upon to test their faith. After the exodus from Egypt, the Children of Israel stood by the shores of the sea and faced one of two choices: to surrender to Pharaoh and the Egyptian army which pursued them, thus returning to bondage and eternal servitude, or to cast their lot with G-d and jump into the sea. Their choice was faith, and when the waters reached their nostrils and they could breathe no more, the Divine intervened, and the sea was split so that they could now walk upon dry land in its midst. At that moment "they believed in Hashem and His servant Moses" (*Shemos* 14:31).

Four hundred years of battles and wars were fought before King David could declare that the entire land of Israel was possessed by the people unto whom G-d had promised it. G-d gave this land to His nation, but it was first necessary that they fight and die for it. Every event in our people's history required extraordinary sacrifice. This is the test by which faith is determined and taught. We succeeded when we bound our sons upon an altar, and in the two-thousand-year exile of our people, we untied those bonds to become the worlds most oppressed nation.

The *Akeidah,* the binding of Yitzchak represented the tying of the very special bond unique to Jews. Yitzchak was to be bound by his father to an altar of total commitment so each successive generation would forge a link with its predecessor, and the *Akeidah,* the quintessential Jewish experience, would continue in perpetuity. Thus, the act of a father offering that which he loves most upon an altar would no longer be necessary. Failing, however, to make this commitment severs the generational link, and a new *akeidah* is needed as a test of faith; thus Egypt pursues Israel, the land that G-d gave us must be fought for. And in modern times, Israel is in a continuous struggle for its survival.

From its very beginning starting with our father Avraham, Judaism was subject to cynical repudiation. It was maintained that religion should **not** require physical commitment and sacrifice. Avraham was scorned when he followed the command to subject himself to a *Bris Milah.* The *Bris,* G-d's covenant with Israel is the quintessential percept of Torah. "Great is *Bris Milah,* since but for that, the Holy One blessed be He, would not have created the universe" (*Nedarim* 31b). The initiation of a Jewish male child to Judaism with the performance of *Bris Milah* is in complete counter- distinction to all other faith systems. G-d demands of Israel **physical** commitment.

The early Christians, as did the founders of Jewish reform, repudiated this practice. Belief, they argued, is a spiritual matter, and this corporal commitment is a contradiction to religion. *Halachah,* however, the Torah way, views spirituality independent of one's **total** being as a vacuous idea.

The child, while he yet bleeds from the physical revision made upon his body is raised up to be named as a Jew, and the words of the prophet Ezekiel are called out: "And I passed by you and saw you wallowing in your blood, and I said to you 'In your blood live,' and I said to you: 'In your blood live' " (*Yechezkel* 16:6), for this is the Divine gift to the people He chose on Mt. Sinai. This unifying thread begins on the eighth day of a Jewish male child's life, and it continues as another link in the *Akeidah* which made of the first Jewish child, Yitzchak, a Jew. By the essence of our lives, the blood of our being, do we as Jews live and upon this altar of faith, do we achieve continuity and blessing.

פרשת חיי שרה
Parshas Chayei Sarah

Rabbi Cyril K. Harris

EXTENDING OUR GOOD WISHES ON HAPPY OCCASIONS AND SHOWERING BLESS-
ings on the joyful celebrants is an integral part of every *Simcha* and
really helps to create the right atmosphere.

At the ceremony of a *Bris,* immediately after the proud father's *Berachah*
on bringing his son "into the Covenant of Abraham," we all shout out
loudly and joyfully: כשם שנכנס לברית כן יכנס לתורה ולחפה ולמעשים טובים —
"*Just as he has entered into the Covenant, so may he enter into the Torah,
the marriage canopy and into good deeds.*"

This time-honored and much-loved wish encapsulates our hopes and
dreams for the newly circumcised infant — first that Torah learning and
values will be the guiding force of his life; second, that when he grows up
he will experience deep contentment in marriage, and finally, that his
future actions will truly benefit the community and society at large.

Beautiful words of blessing must be accompanied by sincerity of heart.
Simply to state the greetings in a perfunctory manner without genuine
feeling and warmth, is to rob the blessing of any validity. We must not be
half-hearted in giving voice to our wishes for the well-being of others but
always mean what we say.

In *Parshas Chayei Sarah,* Rivkah is given the ancient blessing to be
granted offspring — we use it to this day in the ceremony *of Badeken di
Kallah*: אחתנו את היי לאלפי רבבה — "*Our sister may you become the mother*

---

*Rabbi Harris is Chief Rabbi, Union of Orthodox Congregations of South Africa, Johannes-
burg.*

30 ⌒ ENTERING THE COVENANT

of thousands of myriads . . ." (*Bereishis* 24:60).

However, the Midrash tells us that Rivkah's family were somewhat reluctant to let her go, so the blessing was given grudgingly and with an absence of goodwill. Moreover, Rabbi Ze'ev Wolf Einhorn in his commentary on that Midrash asks us to note the order of the words. Instead of blessing Rivkah and then sending her on her way, the text tells us: וישלחו את רבקה אחתם . . . ויברכו את רבקה — *"And they sent their sister Rikvah away . . . And they blessed Rivkah . . ."*

They actually waited until she was outside sitting on the camel, and then almost as an after-thought gave her the blessing, calling it out as she was beginning her journey. The result of such desultory and insincere wishes was that Rivkah was childless. Only when Yaakov entreated Hashem with all his heart, as we are told at the beginning of the next *Parshah,* was Rivkah eventually blessed with children.

Our prayers and blessings on this happy occasion come from the heart. We wish only the best, materially and spiritually, for the new baby boy. Today, as he enters the House of Israel, our good wishes, sincere and well-meant, ring in his little ears, and bring the promise of abundant *nachas* to his dear parents, the entire family, and to *Klal Yisrael.* Indeed, may he grow לתורה ולחפה ולמעשים טובים!

פרשת תולדת
Parshas Toldos

_____ *Rabbi Howard Gershon*

HARAV MOSHE FEINSTEIN, *ZT"L*, OFFERS A NOVEL AND FRESH INTERPRETATION of the opening verse of this week's *Sidrah*: ואלה תולדת יצחק בן אברהם, אברהם הוליד את יצחק — "And these are the offspring of Yitzchak son of Avraham — Avraham begot Yitzchak" (*Bereishis* 25:19). The words "Avraham begot Yitzchak" seem redundant because the verse already stated that Yitzchak was the son of Avraham. Why repeat the seemingly identical piece of information?

Rav Moshe, *zt"l,* explains the separate meanings of the phrases, "the son of Avraham" and "Avraham begot Yitzchak" as follows: Avraham was the paragon of righteousness and *chessed* and Yitzchak loyally followed his example. This is alluded to by the words, "Yitzchak the son of Avraham." Yitzchak was a son who embraced his father's example and who followed exactly in the footsteps of his father — the *Ish Ha'chessed.*

Nevertheless, Yitzchak's educational training and development was not left to chance. Avraham took an active role in Yitzchak's spiritual growth and maturity. This is what the verse indicates with the words, אברהם הוליד את יצחק — "Avraham begot Yitzchak." Avraham was not merely a model for Yitzchak to follow but a father who provided him with proper guidance, as well. Avraham eagerly and enthusiastically assumed the responsibility of educating his son בדרך התורה, in the ways of Torah and figured significantly in molding and shaping Yitzchak's character and personality.

_____

Rabbi Gershon is Executive Director, Adolph Schreiber Hebrew Academy of Rockland, Monsey, New York.

Good role models are essential for a child, therefore, the Torah states, "Yitzchak ben Avraham." However, there must also be the Avraham הוליד את Yitzchak aspect — a father and a mother who are actively involved in their child's upbringing; parents, who teach, supervise and give proper direction to their child.

In a similar approach Rabbi S. R. Hirsch explains the verse in *Tehillim*: כחיצים ביד גבור כן בני הנעורים — "Like arrows in the hand of a warrior, so are the children of youth" (*Tehillim* 127:4).

Concerning the analogy between child rearing and archery, Rabbi Hirsch observes that just as an arrow shot from the bow of a strong archer flies powerfully long after leaving the marksman's hand and follows the straight course set by him, so do children remain true to the direction in which they were guided by their vigorous young parents. The powerful influence of such parents endures long after the children have left the parents' home.

We are confident that you will heed the lessons of Avraham *Avinu* and provide your new son with appropriate guidance and serve as role models for him to emulate. Our hope and prayer is that your instructive and loving "arrows" will find their mark and set him on the course of Torah and *maasim tovim*. May your son be a source of pride and joy to you and may he bring *nachas* to all of *Klal Yisrael*.

פרשת ויצא
Parshas Vayeitzei

_____ *Rabbi Jacob J. Schacter*

ROUD AND EXCITED PARENTS, HAVING JUST CELEBRATED THE BIRTH OF A SON,
experience conflicting emotions. Surely most paramount in their
hearts and minds is the joy they feel and the gratitude they express to G-d
for their new wonderful gift and blessing. But with the joy comes a serious
sense of responsibility, a recognition that they are now charged with that
most important of tasks — raising their son with traditional Jewish ideals
while surrounded by a post-modern world full of values often directly inim-
ical to them. How can they achieve this most significant and vital goal?

The late Rabbi Yaakov Kamenetzky, *zt"l,* offered an outstanding insight
in his *Emes li-Yaakov* commentary on this *parshah.* At the end of the pre-
vous *parshah,* Yitzchak had told his son Yaakov to leave Canaan and his
parental home to go and find a wife from among the members of Rivkah's
family in Padan Aram (*Bereishis* 28:1-4). Our *parshah* tells us that Yaakov
did so and that "He happened *to reach a certain place* where he spent the
night, as the sun had set. He took from the stones of the place and put them
under his head and he laid down *in that place*" (28:11). Rashi notes that the
Torah means to convey that only *there* did he, finally, go to sleep. However,
in the previous fourteen years after having left his home, when he went to
study in the yeshiva of Ever, he was so immersed in Torah study that he did
not sleep.

Reb Yaakov poses the following question: Yaakov was sixty-three years
old when he left home (see *Rashi, Bereishis* 28:9). Prior to that time he had
already been involved in the study of Torah — first, until the age of fifteen,

*Rabbi Schacter is Dean of the Rabbi Joseph B. Soloveitchik Institute in Boston, Massa-
chusetts.*

in the yeshiva of Avraham and, thereafter, in his father's yeshiva (see *Yoma* 28b; *Rambam, Mishneh Torah, Hil. Avodah Zarah* 1:3). But now, after more than six decades of studying Torah, his father charged him with the obligation of finding a wife. What right did he have to stop off for an additional fourteen years at Ever's yeshiva? First of all, what could he learn there that he had not previously learned from his father and grandfather, surely two of the greatest of all teachers? And secondly, what about the *mitzvah* of *kibbud av va-em*? This is comparable, says Reb Yaakov, to a child whose parents ask him to buy them a container of milk and, on his way to the grocery store, he stops off to learn in the *bais midrash* for a few hours. Is now the time for learning? Obey your parents, buy the milk, and *then* go to the *bais midrash*!

Reb Yaakov suggests an explanation crucially important for new parents contemplating the joyous and awesome responsibility that now lies before them. Sure, Yaakov studied the Torah of Avraham and Yitzchak for over half a century. But that Torah was pure Torah, pristine Torah, in-a-perfect-world Torah, in-an-ivory-tower Torah. But how relevant would this Torah be in the base, crass and highly imperfect world of Lavan? No longer would Yaakov be living in the spiritual and exalted world of his father and grandfather. In his new and very far from perfect surroundings, the pristine Torah of the *Avos* could have no place. It was for this reason, says Reb Yaakov, that Yaakov *Avinu* felt the need to study for an additional fourteen years in the Yeshiva of Ever. Only there, under the tutelage of a *rosh yeshiva* raised in the surroundings of the *dor haflagah,* would he be taught how to adapt the Torah of Avraham and Yitzchak to the hostile and material environment of Lavan. What this really resembles, says Reb Yaakov, is a child whose parents ask him to buy them a *lulav* and *esrog*. Not knowing the relevant *halachos,* he firsts closets himself in the *bais midrash* for a few hours and then proceeds on his errand. In this circumstance, the side excursion is crucial to the fulfillment of the parental request. So too, here, says Reb Yaakov. Stopping at the yeshiva of Ever was essential for properly carrying out Yitzchak's initial command.

Dear parents, as you celebrate the birth of your son, remember both parts of Yaakov's training — the pure Torah of his father and grandfather and the applicability of that Torah to the world of Lavan as taught by Ever. Teach both aspects of Torah to your child and with G-d's help, yet another link will be added to the chain of Jewish tradition — from Avraham to Yitzchak, to Yaakov, to your parents, to you, and now, to your child. Mazel Tov.

פרשת וישלח
Parshas Vayishlach

_____ *Rabbi Dr. Moshe Yeres*

A FTER YAAKOV DEPARTS FROM HIS CLIMACTIC MEETING WITH EISAV, THE Torah tells us that Yaakov arrived at the city of Shechem and there built an altar to pray to *HaKadosh Baruch Hu. Perek* 33 concludes: ויקרא לו א־ל אלקי ישראל — "And proclaimed 'G-d, the G-d of Israel' " (33:20). This unusual phrase is what leads *Chazal* in *Maseches Megillah* 18a to interpret it as if G-d Himself called Yaakov קל, a deity, i.e. "He called him קל: who called him this? *Elokei Yisrael.*" The *Midrash Rabbah* paraphrases it slightly differently: אמר אתה אלו־ה בעליונים ואני אלו־ה בתחתונים — Yaakov said [to G-d]: "You are the G-d among the celestial beings and I am the god among the beings of this world." This haughtiness, says the Midrash, did not go unnoticed; and because of it Yaakov was punished with the incident of Dinah, which brought him tremendous anguish.

When one celebrates a *Bris Milah* and commemorates the first *mitzvah* incumbent on a baby, one is filled with a sense of anticipation as to how this young child will turn out. We strive to educate our children so that they will grow up with a sense of values to our Torah and *Yiddishkeit.* If only this child will develop into a *tzaddik,* a truly righteous person, we would be so blessed and thankful. We live in a wonderful age of renewed commitment to *limud HaTorah* and *kiyum ha'mitzvos.* We exist in an era when there appears to be a revitalization of Orthodox Judaism in our midst. Yet at the same time, the concern we maintain for all of *Klal Yisrael* indicates that

_____

Rabbi Dr. Yeres enjoys teaching adults and teenagers. He presently serves as Grade Coordinator at the Community Hebrew Academy of Toronto (CHAT) and on the rabbinic staff of Aish HaTorah, Thornhill, Canada.

while Orthodoxy grows stronger, Jews as a complete community are growing weaker. Numbers do not lie and those who return to Torah are disproportionate to those who have opted out. We are building citadels of Torah, and yet there are those who surround them with a moat of separatism that tells us that we are complacent that most of our people feel cut off from them.

When raising children in Torah, we need to be careful not to create in them a feeling of triumphal superiority over the rest of *Klal Yisrael*. Yes we are proud of their religious growth, and we would be doubly proud if all our children indeed grew up to be *tzaddikim gemurim*. But it is as important that we make them aware of their responsibility to *Klal Yisrael*. We pray to G-d that באורך נראה אור — "By Your light may we see light" (*Tehillim* 36:10). Yet the best *nachas* would be for our children to grow up and serve as an "*or laYehudim,*" to light the way for others to reach Hashem's Torah.

Yaakov's "error," if one may define it as such, was in allowing his sense of *kedushah* to create a feeling of moral and religious superiority. True, G-d made him aware of his special status, but Yaakov allowed himself to lord over others. This is why he was punished with the incident of Dinah.

The Midrash in commenting on the beginning of *Parshas Kedoshim* (*Vayikra* 19:2) states: — דבר אל בני ישראל . . . "קדושים תהיו"; יכול כמוני,ת"ל "כי קדוש אני ה׳. . ." קדושתי למעלה מקדושתכם, "Speak to the Children of Israel. . . 'You shall be holy'; perhaps like Me, the Talmud cites the continuation of the *pasuk* 'for holy am I, Hashem your G-d' . . . My holiness supersedes your holiness." I would suggest that part of what the Midrash is trying to present here is that we can never allow our personal approach to sanctity to remove us from the needs of this world.

Raising a child today is both a challenge and a *nachas*. The *Bris Milah* performed today is done with a *minyan* to indicate the necessity of community. Our prayer is that the upcoming generation will continue to serve as a bridge and convey the message of Hashem and the Torah to all of *Klal Yisrael*.

פרשת וישב
Parshas Vayeishev

_____ *Rabbi Fabian Schonfeld*

T HERE IS A DISPUTE AMONG THE HALACHIC AUTHORITIES AS TO WHETHER THE
blessing of *Shehecheyanu* is recited by the father of the infant son at
the time of the *Bris.* The Sephardic authorities require that the blessing be
recited, whereas Ashkenazic authorities do not require such a *berachah.*
Both are, however, agreed that this dispute applies only to the Diaspora
and that in Eretz Yisrael it is uniformly practiced that the *Shehecheyanu* is
recited even by Ashkenazic families.

The reason why Sephardim recite this *berachah* is quite understandable.
After all, it is a happy occasion and as such *Shehecheyanu* would be very
much in place, no matter where the *Bris* takes place.

Ashkenazi Rabbis agree, but maintain that the *mitzvah* of *Bris Milah*
involves *tzaarei d'yenuka* which means pain felt by the infant. Therefore, it
would not be proper to pronounce the *Shehecheyanu* since the occasion
involves physical discomfort and therefore, *Shehecheyanu* would not be
applicable.

That being the case, why would Ashkenazim agree that in Eretz Yisrael
the *berachah* is appropriate? Does not the child experience pain in Eretz
Yisrael as well? Perhaps the answer is that the term *tzaarei d'yenuka* does
not only refer to the *physical* pain felt by the infant but there is the additional pain of raising him to be an upright and G-d fearing Jew. There is
tzaar gidul banim (the "pains" of parenthood) involved in the process of
one's children's education. Yet we have to understand that if we live in the
Diaspora that pain is much more acute and this point does not require

_____

Rabbi Schonfeld is rav of the Young Israel of Kew Garden Hills, Flushing, New York.

elaboration. On the other hand, in Eretz Yisrael, even in non-observant communities the child would at least be raised as a Jew. True we may wish that he was exposed more to the beauty of Torah and *Mitzvos* than is practiced in secular circles. The fact is, however, that the danger of leaving Jewish identity and possible intermarriage is greatly reduced in Eretz Yisrael. This being so we need not experience the same degree of *tzaar gidul banim* in Eretz Yisrael. Consequently, we are entitled and, indeed, required to say the *berachah* of *Shehecheyanu*. After all, we recite it for new clothing and a new fruit and thus, we should certainly say it for a new Jew.

In the Diaspora that fear of losing one's Jewish identity is real and much more prevalent and threatening, in addition to the matter of *tzaarei d'yenuka*. Therefore, we omit the *berachah* of *Shehecheyanu* in the *Golah*. It is also possible that Sephardic communities do recite it even outside of the Land of Israel because they are a much more insular community that does not have to be as concerned with the loss of Jewish identity. Consequently, they can rightfully recite the *Shehecheyanu*, being confident that the baby will grow up with his Sephardic traditions intact.

In the *parshah* of *Vayeishev* we read of the special love that Yaakov had for Yosef. This love for Yosef, who was his *Ben Zekunim* has been transmitted to us throughout the generations. Our most precious possession and, therefore, our major concern has always been and continues to be our young children. We worry about their education and physical and spiritual well-being.

It is in this spirit that we approach the *mitzvah* of *Bris Milah* and why it is such a moving and sensitive moment in the life cycle of our people.

פרשת מקץ
Parshas Mikeitz

_____ Rabbi Benjamin Blech_

A *Bris* IS A TIME TO DREAM — TO DREAM OF THE FUTURE WHEN זה הקטן גדול יהיה — "may this little one become great." But as we celebrate this wonderful moment, it is the Torah that reminds us so powerfully that there are two kinds of dreamer. There is the dreamer of last week's *Sidrah* and the dreamer of this week's portion. Yosef *HaTzaddik* had dreams and so, too, did Pharaoh, the king of Egypt. But, oh, what a difference between them! And it is in understanding the wide gulf which separates them that we can begin to grasp what we should really pray for on this day.

You remember that Yosef came to his brothers and told them about the sheaves in the field. It was a dream that dealt with produce, with crops and with blessings in a farmer's fields. Clearly its symbolic meaning reflected economic success. It was a vision concentrating on material, earthly matters. Yet it could very well be within the hopes and aspirations of even the most pious person because, as *Chazal* state, אם אין קמח אין תורה — "Without the physical means there can be no spiritual." The striving for bread is a necessary prerequisite for being enabled to study Torah.

Yosef dreamt of sheaves — and it was indeed a prophetic allusion to the great prominence he would attain in the Egyptian court as he saved their economy from ruin and starvation. But what would empower him to rise to the far more significant level of Yosef *HaTzaddik* was the fact that he was not content with one dream but that he pursued with even more diligence

_____

Rabbi Blech is Rabbi Emeritus, Young Israel of Oceanside, Oceanside, New York and Professor of Talmud, James Striar School, Yeshiva University, New York City.

a second. One may strive for success on earth — but a righteous person knows he must also try to reach for the heavens. "And he dreamed yet *another* dream" (*Bereishis* 37:9). This dream was no longer a dream of fields. Now it was his soul that soared close to G-d and took as its subjects the sun, the moon and the stars.

Remarkable, is it not, that to this very day we refer to him by two names — Yosef *HaTzaddik.* His first name relates to the initial dream while the second to the latter. Yosef — he will gather, he will add — represents the "sheaves" of material blessing. *HaTzaddik* — he will remember that all his deeds are inscribed in the heavens above and he will cherish the teachings of his "sun and moon," his beloved father and mother.

The man who had dreams in this week's Torah portion, Pharaoh, called upon the dreamer Yosef (last week's *Sidrah*) to interpret them. Yosef *HaTzaddik* stood before royalty and is commanded to explain the deeper meaning of the king's visions. Not unexpectedly, he is informed that the king also had two dreams. How interesting, he must have said to himself, that's just what happened to me.

But then the king tells him the content of his dreams. He shares with him the details of the first — "seven cows, fat-fleshed and well-favored . . . seven other cows, poor and very ill-favored and lean-fleshed. . . ." (41:18-19). It is meat and food, it is fat and skinny, it is poor and well-to-do. Yes, says Yosef, I understand very well. And now, let me hear the second that will tell me something of your spiritual aspirations in addition to your material concerns. And Pharaoh goes on to tell him about "seven ears came up upon one stalk, full and good, and behold seven ears withered and thin and blasted with the east wind sprung up after them . . ." (41:22-23). Cows and corn. Food and more food. Money and more money. And Yosef understood the difference between his dreams and the dreams of the ruler of Egypt. ויאמר יוסף אל פרעה חלום פרעה אחד הוא — "And Joseph said unto Pharaoh, 'The dream of Pharaoh *is one*'" (41:25).

No you don't have to be Jewish to dream. You only have to be Jewish not to be content with one dream.

Note the number of cows and the number of corn in the dream of the non-Jew. Seven and only seven. The world was created in seven days and I am content with everything that is in the world. Comes the Jew and says NO. My vision is to go beyond what is here. The natural is seven; going beyond it is even better. The earth as we know it is seven; the spiritual meaning which must be added to it to make it worthwhile brings it up to eight. As the *Maharal* put it so beautifully, seven is *Teva* (natural), eight is למעלה מן הטבע (supernatural) — the recognition of eight brings us to the profoundest understanding of the deeper meaning of our lives and the universe.

Therefore, it is no wonder at all that a *Bris* takes place on the eighth day. It is on this very day that we welcome our sons into *Klal Yisrael.* It is our way of expressing this beautiful concept. Yes, we wish for you much material success. The "sheaves" will be yours. But we also want the heavens for you, so that you will reach out to the sky and the stars. May you, our beloved *ben bris,* have the dual blessing of both names of our Biblical hero, *Yosef HaTzaddik.* And just as today you have celebrated your *Bris,* may we live to share with you your growth *to Torah,* *Chuppah,* and *Ma'assim Tovim.*

פרשת ויגש
Parshas Vayigash

Rabbi Yaacov Haber

THE LIFE OF YOSEF SEEMED TO HAVE GONE FROM BAD TO WORSE. IT STARTED off with sibling rivalry, which escalated into being abandoned in a scorpion-infested ditch. He was pulled out of the pit only to be sold to the Yishmaelim, and finally into the hands of the Egyptians. In Egypt, he became a slave in the house of Potifar until wrongfully accused he languished in an Egyptian jail. From his cell, however, life seemed to take a drastic new turn. Yosef was released from jail, and stood as a dignitary before Pharaoh. He became Viceroy of Egypt and was eventually reunited and reconciled with his family. He also reached the ultimate pinnacle of his life when he was able to give peace and sustenance to the entire Jewish people.

We can pinpoint the moment when Yosef's life turned around. It was the moment in his prison cell when Yosef woke up in the morning and looked over at his Egyptian cellmate, a truly guilty convict, and noticed that he wasn't himself. "What is the matter?" asked Yosef "Why do you look so upset today?" Yosef accurately interpreted his dream. Consequently, he was called upon to interpret Pharaoh's dreams. As a result of this encounter he was appointed viceroy of Egypt. From that altruistic moment in prison Yosef suddenly found himself on top of the world. It was at that moment that Yosef's life took on a whole new focus. The moment that his focus shifted outward, towards another human being, success set in. Yosef

Rabbi Haber is the National Director of Jewish Education at the Orthodox Union and Morah D'asrah of Congregation Bais Torah, Monsey, New York.

began his life interpreting his own dreams, and succeeded in life by interpreting other people's dreams.

Today we attend a *Bris.* It is the rite of passage and the very first *mitzvah* this child will do. Interestingly, a child does not enter into the covenant by *receiving* something or by adding something to his person. G-d commands this eight-day-old infant and his parents to *give* something up. The initiation into Judaism is a selfless act. At the *Bris* we charge the child and say, "Just as you entered in the *Bris* with selflessness, so too, will you enter into a life of Torah, *chuppah* and good deeds." The only way to succeed in the process of Torah education is by being willing to make sacrifices and by focusing outward. At the *chuppah* a young man must make a commitment to put someone else first in his life. He can derive from the lesson of the *Bris* how to have a successful marriage. So too, with any good deed, whether it be personal, for his family or for the Jewish people, success is determined by how selfless and willing he is to give something up. We wish the רך הנמול and his parents the fulfillment of the *berachah* of כשם שנכנס לברית. May we all derive much *nachas* from him.

פרשת ויחי
Parshas Vayechi

_____ *Rabbi Raphael B. Butler*

A T THE TIME OF A *BRIS,* ALL THOSE PRESENT EXPRESS THE HOPE OF כשם שנכנס לברית כן יכנס לתורה ולחפה ולמעשים טובים — "Just as the child has entered into the Covenant of *Bris Milah,* so, too, may he nurture his covenantal life through Torah, marriage and good deeds." It is, in fact, an overwhelming *berachah* for a child whose life has just begun. To successfully navigate one's life through the prism of Torah, to marry the appropriate mate and to achieve a life of benevolence for humanity requires far more than just the prayerful expression of family and friends. It needs Divine intervention and support.

In *Parshas Vayechi,* Yaakov *Avinu,* prior to his death, outlines for us the manner in which we can, indeed, become receptacles of *berachah* — the recipients of boundless blessings from God, Himself.

As Yaakov blesses his son, Yosef, he adds that the God who walked with my fathers and, האלקים הרעה אתי — "the God who shepherded me" until this day (*Bereishis* 48:15), המלאך הגאל אתי מכל רע יברך את הנערים — "may the angel who redeemed me from all bad bless [Yosef's] children," Ephraim and Menashe (v.16). What's fascinating in the construction of this verse is the terminology of האלקים הרעה אתי — the God of Judgment who shepherds me. The Sforno says that these words denote the God who acted with me in a manner of *chessed,* kindness. Hashem cared for me even when I was undeserving of His care. Utilizing the Sforno's explanation that the God of Judgment is the God of *chessed;* we

_____

Rabbi Butler is President of Ventures in Jewish Life, New York City..

may note that at times, even when God acts with us in a judgmental manner, it is, indeed, another manifestation of His kindness.

The *Or HaChaim* explains that in the verse, האלקים הרעה אתי, Yaakov is, in fact, establishing the guidelines by which we can merit the world of *berachah*. In order to be a recipient of God's goodness, one must be prepared to follow God as sheep follow a shepherd. Yaakov, therefore, is suggesting to his children and grandchildren that to be worthy of the world of *berachah* and to merit the *chessed* of Hashem, our Shepherd, we must be prepared to act as subserviently as sheep, to follow in the ways of Hashem. Yaakov is teaching us that aside from the *zechus avos* — merits of our forefathers — man's personal merits of uncontested devotion to God will create opportunities for man to, in fact, become recipients of God's boundless kindnesses.

Therefore, at a *Bris,* when we as a community pray that the child develop and follow a life of "*Torah, Chuppah* and *Maasim Tovim,*" the overarching hope is that the child appreciates the relationship necessary to secure these *berachos* of life. It is our hope and our prayer that the child, at the moment of the *Bris,* position himself to always be aware and responsive to God as his Shepherd so that he will act in subservience and devotion to merit Hashem's *chessed.*

Sefer Shemos

פרשת שמות
Parshas Shemos

Dr. Paul Ratzker

IN THIS WEEK'S _PARSHAH_ WE FIND A VERY INTERESTING INTERLUDE IN THE SE-
quence of events. The narration of Moshe's return to Egypt to orches-
trate the יציאת מצרים (Exodus from Egypt) is interrupted by a very brief (3
verses), but poignant vignette: The incident at the מלון, inn.

A _malach_ (angel) accosts Moshe, attempting to kill him. The Midrash
explains that the _malach_ took the form of a serpent. The angel initially
swallowed Moshe from his head to his midsection. Subsequently he swallowed Moshe from his feet to his loins, thus making Tzipporah (Moshe's
wife) understand that it was the issue of the circumcision of their son
Eliezer that imperiled Moshe's life.

In _Meseches Nedarim_, Rabbi Yose explains, that certainly Moshe could
not be guilty of not circumcising his son. Rather, he was faced with a
dilemma. He knew that the baby would be in danger for the first three
days after the _Bris Milah_. Yet, Hashem had commanded him to return to
Egypt. He would be forced to either delay the circumcision, or his journey to Egypt. As God had obviously "known" about the new child, and
still had commanded him to go, Moshe decided to travel immediately.
The question then arises, if this was Moshe's line of reasoning, why was
he held accountable?

Rashi in _Nedarim_ (31b-32a) elucidates the course of events: Upon his
arrival at the inn, Moshe began making lodging arrangements, rather
than immediately performing the _Bris Milah_. We would perceive this as a

Dr. Ratzker is a neurosurgeon residing in Livingston, New Jersey.

rather trivial delay. However, *Tzaddikim* are held to a far higher standard than ordinary individuals. This relatively minor delay placed Moshe's life in jeopardy.

Tzipporah quickly comprehends the situation. She takes a sharp stone and immediately circumcises Eliezer. The *malach* releases Moshe and Tzipporah exclaims, חתן דמים למולות — "A bridegroom's bloodshed was because of circumcision" (*Shemos* 4:26). The רא״ם asks the following question: our understanding of Tzipporah's pronouncement is that Moshe, her "*chassan*," almost lost his life over the circumcision. Yet, didn't she clearly realize this previously? *Gur Aryeh* makes an important distinction. Initially, Tzipporah believed that the *malach* attacked Moshe as *punishment* for delaying the *Bris Milah*. Now she understood that the angel had been *threatening* his life as a means of prompting her to circumcise her son immediately. The actions of the *malach* served to demonstrate to her the supreme importance of the *mitzvah* of *Milah*. Thus, the entire episode underscores to us the tremendous significance Hashem places on this *mitzvah*. It must be performed at the earliest possible opportunity.

The *mitzvah* of *Milah* is central to the Jewish faith. Circumcision is the only immutable physical characteristic that distinguishes us from the people of the world. *Milah* is the only present day positive commandment (מצות עשה) for which the penalty for non-performance is *Kares* (*Korban Pesach* is the only other). It is one of the very few principles delineated for us by Hashem as a *Bris*, a covenant. The core concept behind circumcision is that Hashem intentionally created man in an imperfect state. We are commanded to "complete" the creation of a human being. Therefore, it is imperative that we perform this action as soon as possible.

Today we celebrate the *Bris Milah* of _____. We, too, are performing this *mitzvah* at the earliest opportunity; the morning of the eighth day of his life. This is in the spirit of our enlightened understanding of the episode at the inn. This tradition has been accepted and crystallized throughout the ranks of Judaism. The formal induction of a newborn into *Klal Yisrael* cannot be delayed.

I want to wish the parents and grandparents a hearty Mazel Tov.

פרשת וארא
Parshas Va'eira

_____ *Rabbi Nachum Muschel*

וגם אני שמעתי את נאקת בני ישראל . . . ואזכר את בריתי — "MOREOVER, I HAVE heard the groan of the Children of Israel . . . and I have remembered My covenant" (*Shemos* 6:5). As the *parshah* opens, Hashem reassures Moshe that *Bnai Yisrael*'s redemption from their enslavement in Egypt is sure to come. In fact, it is on its way. Hashem highlights numerous factors, some implicitly, some explicitly, as the reason for this historic, much anticipated emancipation. Among these factors we find the merit of our *Avos* (זכות אבות), the exceeding suffering of the Jewish people (קשי השעבוד), and the outpouring of prayers emanating from the oppressed people (נאקת בני ישראל).

G-d's affirmation to act on His promise to redeem the Jewish people focuses on two additional factors. These may be considered to somehow be associated with the beginning of the life cycle of each Jewish child.

One such factor emphasized the importance of the *Bris,* the covenant that creates a special relationship between Hashem and *Bnei Yisrael.* The words are powerfully clear: ואזכר את בריתי — "I remember my *Bris*" and therefore I am committed to redeem the Jewish people. The second factor emphasizes פדות — distinction, separation — a rather complex concept that is reiterated in the words: ושמתי פדות בין עמי ובין עמך — "I shall make a distinction [separation] between My people and your people" (*Shemos* 8:19).

_____

Rabbi Muschel is Dean Emeritus of Yeshivat Hadar Avraham Tzvi and rav of Congregation Hadar, Monsey, New York.

It is worthy of note that this word פדות appeared in the Torah for the first time with reference to the plague of ערוב. Here, a mixture of different animals and wild beasts attacked the Egyptian nation. It is in reference to this plague that *HaKadosh Baruch Hu* emphasized ושמתי פדות בין עמי ובין עמך — "I will place a separation," or an element of **distinction** "between My people" referring to the Jews, "and your people," referring to the Egyptians. G-d tells Moshe to share this observation with the Jewish people, as well as with the Egyptians. They must know and appreciate the fact that a sign of פדות, of distinction, is essential to the very process of *Yetzias Mitzrayim.*

"There will be a distinct separation between Egyptians and Jews." This separation will even clarify the legal borders of the land of Egypt. Why was it necessary to introduce such a powerful distinction for the first time in this one plague? Distinctions were already observed in the three previous plagues. Yet, no specific emphasis was focused on the aftereffect of each plague that impacted the Egyptians but not the Jews.

Our Biblical interpreters offer an insight worthy of our time. They point out that for the fourth plague — ערוב, G-d brought together animals of all kinds. He smote the Egyptians with a plague that represented a **pluralism** of animals. A conglomeration of all kinds of beasts was assembled for the one and only purpose of attacking the Egyptians. Noting such a miraculous event, one may easily conclude that G-d's preference for pluralism is self-evident. It was necessary, therefore, to caution the Jewish people that, in essence, a conglomeration which is used for a destructive goal is viewed as a plague, rather than a constructive force. It is a *makkah* in its essence, because it serves to attack the Egyptians, but not to strengthen the Jewish people.

Therefore, G-d said to Moshe, as you study the nature of this particular plague, be sure to note the full meaning of the concept פדות, of separation. In this instance, פדות must appropriately be interpreted in Hebrew to mean הבדלה, to make a **distinction,** to pursue an action, the qualities of which characterize the uniqueness of the Jewish people. Both ברית and פדות or פדיון represent such distinction of *Am Yisrael.* Both ברית and פדות endow the Jewish child with the element of קדושה that binds the Jew with *Hakadosh Baruch Hu.* This unique combination proclaims that Jewish greatness and קדושה is through ברית, it is פדות or פדיון, it is הבדלה all in one.

Interestingly, in other contexts the word פדות is used not to connote distinction, but rather to connote גאולה, redemption. פדות שלח לעמו — "He sent redemption to His nation" is a verse in *Tehillim* (111:9) that speaks about גאולה that G-d dispatched to His people. A similar verse in *Tehillim* (130:7) states: והרבה עמו פדות — "and with Him is abundant redemption" and suggests the quality of greatness of true freedom which Hashem deeded to the Jewish people.

A powerful equation emerges for us to ponder and cherish. הבדלה equals גאולה: ואבדיל אתכם מן העמים להיות לי — "I separated you from the rest of the nations. I endowed you with a distinction to be Mine." Thus, we see פדות on one hand associated with הבדלה, and on the other hand it is associated with גאולה. Clearly, to build Jewish life, to foster Jewish continuity one has an obligation to recognize that Jewish strength lies in Jewish distinction. The call goes out to every Jewish parent: Imprint this distinction on your Jewish child beginning with his very birth. Beware, says G-d, of pluralistic waves that seek to overwhelm the Jew, to break the barriers of separation, and to drown out the uniqueness of *Am Yisrael* and undermine our people's claim to eternity.

Jewish continuity, Jewish strength starts at the very beginning of the life cycle of the Jewish child. אשר קדש ידיד מבטן — We thank G-d "for sanctifying our beloved offspring from the moment of birth." Pointedly, the words recorded in *Parshas Shemos* (1:16) contain this hidden message: וראיתן על האבנים אם בן הוא — "Cast your sight at the moment of birth if it is a son." If it is a son with whom G-d has blessed you, then you must do your share to offset every attempt to cause his disappearance from Jewish society. To this end, it is imperative to append to that first look the act of ושמתי פדות.

Build distinctions, protective enclaves around your children where the onslaught of a blend of corruptive influences will stop before reaching your home. This kind of פדות will eventually enable you to attain פדות שלח לעמו, to find the road over which the redemption will be forthcoming to His/our people. It will guide us to a communal redemption attained through greatness and spiritual strength of each individual בן ישראל. It will be a פדות highlighting personal redemption, personal growth, and personal joy associated with each Jewish child in the community as described in the words: והרבה עמו פדות.

Perhaps this is the *berachah* implied in the words זה הקטן גדול יהיה — "May this little one become great." Invent a tiny bit of הבדלה now, and you will harvest a sizable portion of גאולה. וכן יהי רצון.

פרשת בא
Parshas Bo

Rabbi Moshe E. Bomzer

Rav Aharon Soloveitchik teaches us that the _mitzvah_ of _Bris Milah_ consists of two unique aspects or "_Kiyumim._" First there is the aspect of כריתת הערלה — "removing the foreskin," and then there is an additional _Kiyum_ of הטפת דם ברית —"the letting of blood during the process of removing the foreskin."

Rav Aharon continues and suggests that these two factors represent two approaches to our world. The removal of the foreskin parallels the physical world and directs man to remove the imperfect aspects and harness the physical for proper spiritual development. The second, the letting of blood corresponds to the spiritual commitment of the Jew to G-d, the covenantal bond between man and Hashem as stated: אם לא בריתי יומם ולילה חוקת שמים וארץ שמתי — "If not for the blood of the covenant, heaven and earth would not endure" (_Yirmiyahu_ 33:25), and the verse from _Yechezkel_ (16:6) which we state at every _Bris Milah_: ואעבר עליך ואראך מתבוססת בדמיך ואמר לך בדמיך חיי ואמר לך בדמיך חיי — "And when I passed over you and saw you wallowing in your blood. I said to you — 'In your blood live' and I said to you 'In your blood live.' "

These two binding commitments to harness the physical and to dedicate oneself to the spiritual are inextricably bound to the essence of _Yetzias Mitzrayim_ as presented in _Parshas Bo_. For the Jew to succeed in leaving Egypt he, too, needed a double bond contract. The Midrash states on the _pasuk_, (_Shemos_ 12:21) "Moshe called to all the elders of

---

Rabbi Bomzer is rav of Congregation Beth Abraham-Jacob in Albany, New York.

Israel and said to them 'Draw forth (משכו) or buy (קחו) for yourselves one of the flock for your families and slaughter the Pesach offering.' " The Midrash states on the word משכו — pull yourself away from your past — from idolatry, from slavery, and קחו — take on a new role of being G-d's people, of carrying out G-d's *Mitzvos*. In fact the next *pasuk* states that the Jews of the "Exodus" were to take the blood of the paschal lamb and place it on both doorways of their home. Rabbi Samson Raphael Hirsch compares these two doorways to the two covenants. There is the doorway of the physical world and the entranceway into the spiritual world. For the Jew of the Exodus it was necessary to establish both covenantal bonds before the Exodus would be complete. And Yechezkel's words, "in your blood [you will] live" repeated twice has been interpreted to mean the blood of *Bris Milah* and the *blood of the paschal lamb,* and had to be presented on the night of the Exodus. The blood of the lamb represented the spiritual world of dedication to G-d and the blood of *Milah* represented the physical world and the need to let go of all old habits.

Rav Aharon sums up this theme by describing the double bond of Judaism's commitment to its national identity which is spiritual in nature and its universal commitment which is manifested in the physical world of *chesed* and *rachamim* —kindness and compassion.

As you bring your son, grandson, great-grandson to the *mitzvah* of *Milah* our blessing to you is that the covenants of Avraham, and the commitments of Moshe, as well as the ultimate contracts of Yechezkel will be carried on by this little baby boy. May he aspire to harness the physical world around him, whether it be in the laboratory, business or more importantly in the world of kindness and compassion. May his guiding force be the covenant of הטפת דם — to be spiritually bound to Hashem and His *mitzvos* even if it requires the ultimate in sacrifice. Our *tefillah* is that you continue to *see nachas, berachah, mazel* and *hatzlachah* and merit the fulfillment of the *berachos* of *Torah, Chuppah* and *Maasim Tovim.* May Hashem bless him to see the *Dam Milah* and the *Dam Korban Pesach* eternally upon his doorposts.

פרשת בשלח
Parshas Beshalach

_____ _Marcel Weber_

Iɴ PARSHAS BESHALACH WE READ SHIRAS HA'YAM — THE SONG OF THE SEA.
Moshe and _Klal Yisrael_ express great thanks, _Hakoras Ha'tov,_ and
profound _emunah,_ belief, in Hashem. One of the striking phrases, highlighting this commitment to G-d in the _Shira_ is: זה א-לי ואנוהו אלקי אבי
וארממנהו — "This is my God, I will glorify Him. The G-d of my father, I will
exalt Him" (_Shemos_ 15:2). First G-d is praised on a personal level — "my
G-d" — but there is also the glorification of Hashem as the G-d of our
forefathers, our ancestors, אלקי אבי.

Rashi notes this striking duality and comments that _Bnei Yisrael_ is
actually saying: לא אני תחלת הקדושה אלא מוחזקת ועומדת לי הקדושה ואלהותי עלי
מימי אבותי — "I (_Am Yisrael_), today, am not the source of _Kedushah_ —
holiness or commitment to Hashem. Rather, the concept of _Kedushah,_
which I maintain and perpetuate had been established through Hashem's
relationship with my forefathers."

This connection is clearly seen at the ceremony of _Bris Milah._ When we
celebrate the _Bris_ of an infant, we seek the source of the meaning and the
significance of this _Bris_ — this covenant between G-d and the child. Rav
Hutner, in his classic work, _Pachad Yitzchak_ discusses the dual nature
and meaning of the _Bris_ as a personal covenant — זה א-לי ואנוהו , and also
as a covenant entered through our forefathers — אלקי אבי וארממנהו.

Two blessings are recited at the _Bris._ The first blessing is אשר קדשנו. . .

_____

_Mr. Weber is partner in the law firm of Feder, Kaszovitz, Isaacson, Weber & Skala and
immediate past Chairman of the Board of the Orthodox Union._

במצותיו וצונו על המילה — "Blessed are You Hashem, our G-d, King of the Universe, who has sanctified us with His commandments and commanded us to perform the circumcision."

The Torah itself, in describing significant episodes in Avraham's life, reflects on his commitment to the covenant of *Chessed* between man and man. On the third day following his *Bris*, Avraham sits on the doorstep of his home, mid-day, eagerly awaiting guests that he could invite into his home. The "*Shechinah*," the presence of G-d, is visiting him because he is recovering from his *Bris Milah*. Avraham leaves the presence of G-d and rushes to welcome total strangers. The Rabbis, in discussing this episode derive the lesson that welcoming people into one's home (*hachnasas orchim*) is even greater than receiving the presence of G-d — the *Shechinah*. Avraham's whole nature is one of "*Chessed*."

The act of *Bris Milah* itself centers on the male infant's entrance into Avraham's covenant of *Chessed*. We continue the *Mesores*, the tradition that began with our father Avraham. In *Gemara Avodah Zarah* (7b), we learn: "One who is not committed to performing acts of kindness is compared to one who has no G-d"— מי שאינו עוסק בגמילות חסדים דומה למי שאין לו אלו־ה.

Rav Hutner tells us that just as man cannot exist without the kindness of our Creator who is *Gomayl Chassadim*," similarly Hashem will not and cannot be present without man's kindness to man.

When the Torah was given to *Am Yisrael*, they said "*Na-aseh V'nishma*" — "We will do . . . and we will listen", two acts which really are two aspects of a *mitzvah*. The first aspect of a *mitzvah* is נעשה, the physical act of the *mitzvah* itself; its performance. The second aspect is the נשמע. This is the major meaning and purpose implicit in the *mitzvah*.

The act of performing the *mitzvah* is a personal one — זה א־לי ואנוהו,"This is my G-d, I will glorify Him." It involves only the person performing the *mitzvah*.

The second blessing is: ...אשר קדשנו במצונו וצונו להכניסו בבריתו של אברהם אבינו — "Blessed are You, Hashem, our G-d, King of the Universe, who has sanctified us with His commandments and commanded us to enter him (this child) into the covenant of our forefather Abraham." Why is it necessary to have two blessings, both of which appear to refer to the identical act of performing the *Bris*?

Rav Hutner responds that the *mitzvah* of *Milah* contains two distinct aspects. The first blessing is recited on the מעשה המצוה, the actual act of the *mitzvah,* and, accordingly, as the physical act of *Bris* is performed one recites the first *berachah* על המילה, which refers to the physical act of performing *Bris Milah.* Rav Hutner explains that there is a separate dimension and aspect to the *mitzvah* which is encompassed by the second blessing להכניסו בבריתו של אברהם אבינו — "to enter him into the covenant of our forefather Abraham."

At the *Bris,* the child is entered into the *bris* of our forefather Avraham. What does this mean? The covenant that Avraham first observed was that of *Chessed* — he epitomized kindness. The *Gemara* (*Kesubos* 8b) cites a statement of *Chessed* that was recited in ancient times to a mourner: "Our brothers who do bestow deeds of kindness, are the sons of those who perform deeds of kindness, all who uphold the covenant of Abraham, our forefather — the covenant of *Chessed.* "

Every Jewish infant who is given a *bris* is also entered into the covenant of *Chessed.* This then is the separate and distinct blessing entered into, and bestowed by G-d upon Avraham and each of his descendants.

May the רך הנמול merit to continue his dual association with *mitzvos* that he began today. We hope and pray that the parents, grandparents and entire family will have much *nachas* and *birchas kol tuv.*

פרשת יתרו
Parshas Yisro

_____ *Elliot Ganchrow*

I MMEDIATELY FOLLOWING THE EXODUS FROM EGYPT, YISRO COMES WITH THE rest of Moshe's family to join the newly liberated Jewish nation. Moshe tells Yisro of the great miracles —including the splitting of the Red Sea and the war with Amalek which Hashem performed for the Jews on their way out of Egypt. In response to these events the Torah tells us: ויחד יתרו על כל הטובה אשר עשה ה' לישראל אשר הצילו מיד מצרים — "Yisro rejoiced over all the good that Hashem had done for Israel, that He rescued it from the hand of Egypt" (*Shemos* 18:9). The word ויחד is not a word which is frequently used in the Torah. Therefore, *Chazal* offer a number of explanations as to what the Torah means by it. One explanation is that it means joy, and is *Aramaic* in origin. *Chazal* interpret this to mean that after hearing of the great miracles performed by Hashem, Yisro circumcised himself. The question, is why did Yisro, at this point in time, feel a need to circumcise himself?

The *Chasam Sofer*, (as adapted by Rabbi Yosef Stern) gives two possible explanations. First, Yisro was about to partake in sacrifices offered to Hashem and Yisro realized that an uncircumcised person is not allowed to bring and certainly may not eat from sacrificial offerings. Yisro, therefore, circumcised himself prior to bringing the offering (an *olah*) brought by all new converts and *zevachim,* feast offerings to express his gratitude to Hashem.

However, another possible explanation brought down by the *Chasam*

Mr. Ganchrow is an attorney at Paul Hastings, Janofsky, and Walker in New York City.

Sofer is that Moshe told Yisro that the Jews circumcised themselves on the night of the Exodus from Egypt. This fact can be deduced from the previous verse which states, 'את כל התלאה אשר מצאתם בדרך ויצלם ה — "All the travail that had befallen them on the way, and Hashem rescued them" (18:8). This verse is referring to the great strain that the Jews suffered as a result of having to travel immediately after undergoing a circumcision. Nevertheless, the Jews weathered this great burden, with the help of Hashem. Upon being told of the great personal sacrifice which the Jewish people had endured, Yisro realized that he too needed to be circumcised in order to truly join the community of Israel. Thus, this act of circumcision by Yisro represented a great selflessness and commitment on his part, which allowed him to become a member of the Jewish people.

Yisro understood that he could not be a *ben Torah* without performing a *bris.* He realized the importance of accepting the covenant with Hashem that the rest of the nation had already accepted. This dedication to Hashem on the part of Yisro can be seen in the choice of different names which the Torah calls Yisro from time to time. The primary name Yisro, which the Torah calls him most often, means overflowing with good deeds. He is also called "Chovev" which means beloved son of G-d, as well as Pituel, which means he renounced idol worship. These names are proof that the covenant which Yisro had accepted with Hashem was a crucial one.

Today , as we perform the same *bris* that every Jew, as well as Yisro, performed and give the newborn a name which he will have for life, we recall from Yisro the importance which is attached to both of these acts. May this act of the *bris,* as well as the naming of the child serve as an inspiration to his parents, his family, and all of Israel. Mazel Tov.

פרשת משפטים
Parshas Mishpatim

_____ *Rabbi Dr. Herbert C. Dobrinsky*

I WOULD LIKE TO SHARE WITH YOU A BEAUTIFUL INTERPRETATION OF THIS WEEK'S *parshah* developed by Rabbi Osher Anshel Katz of Brooklyn, New York, in his *sefer Nachal Ha-Bris* (published 1964), in the section entitled *Zichron Zvi* — novellae on some of the *parshios* — which I have elaborated upon and amplified.

In Chapter 23 of *Mishpatim,* the Torah instructs us in the manner by which a judge must maintain his integrity. It states: ולא תענה על ריב לנטת אחרי רבים להטת — "Do not be a follower of the majority for evil and do not respond to a grievance by yielding to the majority to pervert the law" (23:2).

Our *Chazal* offer many interpretations, as expounded by Rashi. But one of them is that *you should follow the majority to do good* — meaning that to acquit someone you need only a majority of one, whereas to convict you need a majority of at least two judges.

In connection with the concept of following the majority, the *Midrash Rabbah* (*Vayikra* 4:6) tells us about a non-Jew who asked Rabbi Yehoshua ben Karcha: *"It is written in your Torah:* אחרי רבים להטת — *'you should follow the majority.' Why, therefore, do you not join us in worshipping idolatry, since we are more numerous than you?"* Responded Rabbi Yehoshua ben Karcha: *"Do you have children?"* The gentile replied: *"Yes, and you have reminded me of my trouble."* *"Why?"* asked Rabbi Yehoshua. The

_____
Rabbi Dr. Dobrinsky is vice president for university affairs at Yeshiva University in New York City.

gentile replied: *"I have many children. When they sit at my table one blasphemes the god of the other and they do not rise from the table before they have cracked each other's skulls."* Asked Rabbi Yehoshua: *"And do you bring about agreement among your children?"* *"No"*, was the answer. *"Well then,"* said Rabbi Yehoshua ben Karcha, *"before you make us agree with you, go and bring about agreement among your children."* Thus rebuffed, the heathen went away.

The Rabbis explained, the majority declared by the heathens is simply not true. Because the heathens have so many different deities one can never assess how many adherents follow a specific form of idolatry, whereas we Jews, on the other hand, have only One G-d, and all of us follow Him, and Him alone.

Nevertheless, we still have the question of the *Minim* to answer, namely, why are the Jewish people not בטל ברוב — absorbed into the majority? A possible answer is to be found in *Yoreh Deiah,* where we learn the intricacies of the laws of majority — *rov* — as they apply to kosher meat. We have a law: In a situation when a forbidden piece of meat is attached to a piece of kosher meat, in order for the kosher meat to be usable it has to constitute a *majority* not just in relation to the forbidden piece, but it must be enough to be a *majority* of the *entire* piece to which it is attached. This example may answer the question of why the Jews do not conform to the majority of the gentile world. It is because the Jewish people is inseparably attached — דבוק — to G-d Himself. Consequently, it cannot be governed by general rules of the minority following the majority, since Hashem, to Whom we cling, cannot be overcome by a majority, even as it is stated: אתם הדבקים בה' אלקיכם חיים כלכם היום — "You who cling to Hashem your G-d, you are all alive today" — which the Rabbis explained to mean: רשעים בחייהם קרואים מתים — "the wicked even in their lifetime are called dead," and because we, the Jewish people, are attached to the Almighty we are not absorbed amongst the heathen nations who are wicked and thus considered as dead, but אנו קרואים חיים — "we are called living!"

The important aspect of this is that the דבקות — the attachment of *Bnei Yisrael* to Hashem — is realized specifically through the *mitzvah* of *Milah,* for with this *mitzvah* the Divine stamp and name of G-d is upon the Jew, and through this permanent attachment, he can cling to G-d. This answer is how Hashem also calmed Moshe *Rabbeinu,* who feared that the seventy nations may be a majority to swallow up the Jewish people (*see Yalkut Shimoni, Parshas Tetzaveh, siman* 376).

And it is for the reason of our דבקות בה' alone that the question of the heathen to Rabbi Yehoshua ben Karcha is answered. For us Jews the answer has always been that we can **never** be absorbed by the majority, because through the *mitzvah* of circumcision — *Milah* — we are attached to G-d Himself. As we have already noted from the laws in *Yoreh Deiah,* the majority must also be large enough to overcome that to which the substance in question is attached — דבוק — which in this case is The Holy One, Himself, who cannot be overruled by a majority. Thus, we remain as a unique nation — *"For they are a nation that stands alone and are not counted among the other nations; who has counted the dust of Jacob or numbered the stock of Israel?"* (*Bamidbar* 23:9-10). (Thus concludes a portion of Rabbi Osher Anshel Katz's magnificent explanation, which I am pleased to share with you in translation, with his permission.)

We may recall an incident in the *Tanach* where one prophet, Eliyahu, who was G-d's true prophet, overcame hundreds of false prophets of idolatry (Baal). This biblical epic shows us that if a majority wants to do evil, it will never accomplish its goal. It is, therefore, significant that it is the selfsame Eliyahu who plays such a singular role at every circumcision because he complained to G-d (*Melachim* 1, 19:10): *"I have been very jealous for the L-rd, the G-d of hosts, for the Children of Israel have forsaken Your covenant, etc."* According to the Midrash, Hashem replied to Eliyahu, *"As you live, because of your excessive zeal for Me, whereby you have brought charges against Israel that they have forsaken My covenant, therefore you shall have to be present at every circumcision ceremony wherever my sons shall imprint this sign upon their flesh, so that the mouth which charged Israel with forsaking the covenant shall testify that they are observing it"* (*Zohar, Bereishis* 93a). Also, since the messenger (angel) of the covenant — *Malach HaBris* — mentioned in *Malachi* 3:1, was identified as Eliyahu, it was deemed proper that the "Angel of the Covenant" should be present whenever a Jewish child was circumcised as he entered the Covenant of Abraham. Thus we have the כסא של אליהו — Eliyahu's chair — which is used at the *Bris Milah* ceremony in accordance with the various customs related to it which represents Eliyahu's presence at every circumcision. For as Rabbi Abba taught, when a man takes up his son to initiate him into this covenant, G-d calls to the ministering angels and says: "*See what a creature I have made in the world!*" At that moment, Eliyahu traverses the world in four sweeps and presents himself there, and for this reason we have been taught, it behooves the father of the child to prepare an extra chair in Eliyahu's honor, and to say, "This is the Chair of Eliyahu". If he neglects to do so, Eliyahu does not visit him, or testify to Hashem that the circumcision has taken place (*Zohar, Bereishis* 93a).

All of us, therefore, pray that the רך הנמול — the circumcised infant — this new member of the Jewish people (include the boy's Hebrew name here) may grow to be a source of singular accomplishments on behalf of his people. May he always cling to the teachers of the One True G-d, and not fear those who despite their vast numbers try to divert him from ה׳ אחד — the One and only True G-d. May he be a source of *nachas* to his family as a *ben Torah,* who will bring honor to himself and his people throughout the years ahead as he attains *Torah, Chuppah,* and *Maasim Tovim* to 120 years and clings to Hashem!

פרשת תרומה
Parshas Terumah

_____ *Rabbi David Kaminetsky*

T HE TORAH TELLS US THAT AVRAHAM *AVINU* WAS NOT COMPLETE UNTIL HE WAS
given the *mitzvah* of *Milah*. As the Torah states, התהלך לפני והיה
תמים — "Go before Me and become complete" (*Bereishis* 17:1). There are
many interpretations as to what Hashem meant when He said that Avraham would only be complete once he performs the *mitzvah* of *Milah*.
Among these is the idea that the *Milah* transforms the body from something that is purely physical to something which is spiritual as well. By
removing the foreskin from the body of the eight day old male we are
making a permanent mark on the child's body. We demonstrate that man
must control his thoughts and his desires. This permanent mark will remind the male that the act of cohabitation, which is a physical act, must be
connected with the spiritual. The body and soul are fused together. The
very act through which man procreates and produces his offspring must be
associated with the spiritual. In this way man extends that spirituality to his
children and they to theirs and to future generations.

In *Parshas Terumah* we begin to study the intricate details that were
involved in the construction of the *Mishkan*. Hashem tells us, ועשו לי מקדש
ושכנתי בתוכם — "They shall make for Me a Sanctuary and I will dwell
among them (the Jewish people)" (*Shemos* 25:8).

In this Tabernacle we are instructed to place an ark, a table, a cande-
labra, and a whole selection of other items which we use to serve Hashem.

_____

*Rabbi Kaminetsky is National Director, National Conference of Synagogue Youth
(NCSY), of the Orthodox Union.*

We are told to bring fifteen different types of raw materials, such as gold, silver, copper, etc. to build the Tabernacle and all of its vessels. We are instructed in minute detail how these items are to be constructed. When they are finally completed we are given a detailed review of the construction in a manner that at times appears to be repetitive.

The questions are obvious. Why does Hashem need a physical structure? Why was it necessary for the Jewish people to bring so many different items to be used in the construction and why is the information repeated in detail after the construction was completed? The answer to these questions is that Hashem is giving the Jewish people an opportunity to create holiness in their lives by taking their physical possessions, sanctifying them, and using them to serve Him. He doesn't need the Temple. *We* need it as a place to serve Him. According to many of the commentaries the reason Hashem commanded us to build the Tabernacle is to give us an opportunity to atone for the sin of the golden calf. Just as the Jews gave of their possessions inappropriately for the golden calf so, too, must they now demonstrate their willingness to give of their possessions for a just and holy cause.

We are told to build a Sanctuary so that Hashem may dwell in our midst. In essence we are being asked to bring the spirituality of Hashem into our lives. We are being asked to recognize that all of one's physical possessions ultimately belong to Hashem and are therefore to be used to serve Him. בלבבי משכן אבנה, "In my heart I build a sanctuary." I build the sanctuary in my heart by bringing Hashem's Holiness to everything that I do. This is the message of *Milah* as well. By performing the mitzvah of *Milah* we transform the physical body into something holy. We infuse the body with spirituality and we make sure that that spirituality has the potential to be transferred to future generations. For, the very organ that is used to procreate is the organ that receives this permanent mark of spirituality.

These comparisons can be taken further. The Jewish people took the *Mishkan* with them wherever they traveled. They took the holiness of Sinai with them wherever they went. In this way they were always connected to Sinai. So, too, the *Bris Milah* is a permanent mark which constantly reminds the Jew of his spirituality wherever he is.

May the רך הנמול merit to carry these dual messages of *Milah* and *Mishkan* wherever he goes throughout his life. Our *tefilah* is that he will succeed in this mission and be a source of *nachas* to his family and all of *Klal Yisrael*.

פרשת תצוה
Parshas Tetzaveh

Rabbi Steven Pruzansky

*T*ETZAVEH IS WELL-KNOWN AS THE ONLY *PARSHAH* IN WHICH MOSHE *RABBEINU'S* name is not explicitly mentioned. Instead of the familiar phrase, "And G-d spoke to Moshe, saying . . .", the *sidrah* begins with a command in the second person: "And you . . .." The *Ba'al HaTurim* explains that, in pleading for Divine forgiveness for the sin of the golden calf in next week's *sidrah,* Moshe stated: "And now, if You but forgive their sin! — but if not, erase me now from this book that You have written" (*Shemos* 32:32). Moshe's conditional plea — to be erased from G-d's book — was granted in a limited way; his name was deleted from the *sidrah* of *Tetzaveh.*

Nevertheless, as the *Ba'al HaTurim* himself notes, *Tetzaveh* is *not* the only *sidrah* which omits Moshe's name. There are four *sidros* in the book of *Devarim* which contain no personal reference to Moshe: *Eikev, Re'eh, Shoftim* and *Ki Seitzei.* And yet, the omission of Moshe's name in *Mishneh Torah* attracts little attention. What, then, is the difference between the omission in *Tetzaveh* and those in *Sefer Devarim*?

The answer is that a name symbolizes an identity, a place in the world. Rabbi Samson Raphael Hirsch (Commentary to *Bereishis* 2:19) perceived the root of שֵׁם — a name, as originating in the word שָׁם — there. A name provides a sense of "there", of who and where a person is, a designation by which others will recognize him.

There are two ways in which people are able to forge such an identity. One is through their own words and deeds. They are unmistakably known

Rabbi Pruzansky is rav of Congregation Bnai Yeshurun, Teaneck, New Jersey.

through their accomplishments, actions and statements, and literally "make their own name." This is the Moshe of *Sefer Devarim* — he was the speaker and the principal figure. Everything in those *sidros* reflected the words and deeds of Moshe; he need not be identified or explicitly mentioned in order for the reader to ascertain his presence.

The other way in which people become known is by the name someone else calls them. They are defined by another, an outsider. In such an instance, an ambiguous reference to an individual in the second person (as in our *sidrah,* "And you shall command . . .") *is* a puzzling omission. And so the commentators hasten to explain why Hashem chose to address Moshe using a pronoun, and why Moshe's name does not appear in *Tetzaveh.*

The Jewish child receives his name at the time of his *Bris Milah,* in commemoration of Avraham *Avinu* who was re-named by Hashem on the day of his circumcision. The child's name will be his designation, a statement about who he is and the family from which he comes. "And his name will be called in Israel . . . " — it is the name which will accompany him through the cycles of life as a member of the Jewish nation. Today, the day on which his body receives the imprint of his Jewishness and stamps him as a descendant of Avraham, he is also *given* a name, and a Jewish identity. Now the process starts by which the child will create his *own* name, much as his family has done — a family who have made their name in Torah study, commitment to *mitzvos,* and acts of *chessed.*

May the young child follow in his parents' footsteps and achieve a great name in Israel, and be a source of *nachas* to his family and all Israel.

פרשת כי תשא
Parshas Ki Sisa

_____ *Rabbi Yehoshua Balkany*

T HE *MITZVAH* OF *MILAH* HAS SERVED AS A POWERFUL FORCE, BINDING THE JEW to his Creator with ties that cannot be severed. Thus strengthened, the Jew can overcome the greatest obstacles and spiritual battles — for the covenant between himself and Hashem is everlasting. This explains why, over thousands of years, every regime wishing to wage a war against the Jews has started by imposing the prohibition of *Milah.*

A defining, albeit infamous, moment in the history of *Klal Yisrael* was the sin of the עגל הזהב, the golden calf. How could *Bnai Yisrael* distance themselves from Hashem with such a flagrant act? It was able to happen because they lacked a certain spiritual sensitivity — they did not have *Bris Milah.* Pharaoh had foreseen evil befalling the Jews when he said, כי רעה נגד פניכם — "The evil intent is opposite your faces" (*Shemos* 10:10). The numerical value of רעה is 305, the same as the word ערלה. The רעה that would befall them would stem from their lack of observing the *mitzvah* of *Milah.*

We find this concept of negative repercussion for ignoring the *mitzvah* of *Milah* in Yechezkel as well. There the prophet says, referring to Esav, "Because you have spurned blood, blood shall then pursue you" (*Yechezkel* 35:6). One of Rashi's explanations says that דם שנאת (spurned blood) refers to the blood of *Milah* that Esav rejected. Rejecting a *bris* paved the way for Esav's future evil actions.

Returning to the חטא העגל, we find that Moshe feared Hashem would

_____

Rabbi Balkany is Dean, Bais Yaakov of Brooklyn, New York.

vent His wrath upon the Jews: כי יגורתי מפני האף והחמה —"for I feared the anger and the wrath" (*Devarim* 9:19). He knew Hashem's anger was connected to the *Milah* for the same terminology appears when Moshe delayed performing *Milah* on his own son. It says in Gemara *Nedarim* (32a) that when Moshe *Rabbeinu* delayed his son's *bris* "the avenging angels, *Af V'chaima*, (אף וחמה), came and threatened his very life."

Upon witnessing the Jews worshipping the golden calf, Moshe hurled down the *Luchos* which he had just received from Hashem. The *Chachamim* say that Moshe arrived at this drastic decision by noting the following: In the laws of *korbon Pesach* an "*arel*"—an uncircumcised person — may not take part in the *mitzvah*. If an *arel* (ערל) is excluded from *Pesach*, which is only one *mitzvah*, Moshe reasoned, then surely the entire Torah cannot be given to Jews who are *areilim*.

Moshe stood at the gate of the camp and cried out, מי לה׳ אלי — "Whoever is on G-d's side should join me!" (*Shemos* 32:26), immediately all the Levites gathered around him. Moshe tells each man to place his sword by his side — שימו איש חרבו על ירכו — "every man shall place his sword on his thigh" (v.27) and to kill those who participated in the חטא. The *bnai* Levi joined Moshe because they alone had refrained from sinning with the *egel*. The *Sifsei Kohanim Al HaTorah* notes that they did not sin because they had undergone *Milah*. The letters in the words מי לה׳ also spell מילה, circumcision. The *Leviim* fulfilled the *pasuk* כי שמרו אמרתך ובריתך ינצרו — "They observed Your word and kept Your covenant" (*Devarim* 33:9) — the covenant of *Milah*.

After Hashem forgives the Jews for the *chet ha'egel* we read הנה אנכי כרת ברית — "Behold! I seal a covenant" (*Shemos* 34:10). Hashem and *Bnai Yisrael* renew their covenant, the performance of *Milah*. The *Migdal Oz* of Rabbi Yaakov Emden quotes a *medrash* that translates שימו איש חרבו על ירכו as referring to *Bris Milah*. By abandoning the status of *areilim*, *Bnai Yisrael* could come closer to Hashem through their *teshuvah*. It says that משה מל, אהרן פורע ויהושע משקה — "Moshe performed the *Milah*, Aharon did *preah* and Yehoshua offered *kos shel berachah* to all the circumcised." And Moshe instructs them: מלאו ידכם היום לה׳ כי איש בבנו ובאחיו ולתת עליכם היום ברכה — "Dedicate yourselves today to Hashem for each has opposed his son and his brother that He may bestow upon you a blessing this day" (*Shemos* 32:29).When *Bnai Yisrael* fulfill the *mitzvah* of *Milah*, they bind themselves closer to Hashem, beginning a path of *teshuvah* and *maasim tovim* that can only lead to success and *berachah*.

Our *berachah* to the newborn and his parents is that they will raise their son to be close to Hashem through Torah and *Mitzvos*. Beginning today, with the *mitzvah* of *Milah,* may he continue on this road and become a *ben Torah*. Mazel Tov!

פרשת ויקהל
Parshas Vayakheil

_____ *Rabbi Moshe Elefant*

THE FAMED MAHARSHA HAD A LARGE YESHIVA IN THE TOWN OF OSTRO. AS THE prestige of the institution grew, many students from throughout Europe wanted to attend; however, there were space limitations. Consequently, the Board of Directors of the school decided to build a new edifice, which would be large enough to accommodate the many applicants. Following the custom of the times a festive groundbreaking was planned, with many dignitaries attending. As a means of raising funds for this great undertaking, the privilege of laying the first brick was to be auctioned.

A simple modest Jew approached the auctioneer, informing him that he would like to purchase this honor at any cost. He cautioned, however, that he must insist that no one know that he was the buyer. The selling began and the honor was sold for five hundred rubles, a phenomenal sum in those days. Naturally, all the attendees were curious as to the identity of the benefactor. The auctioneer approached the donor surreptitiously asking him if he would lay the cornerstone. He responded that he was honoring the Maharsha with this privilege, thereby protecting his anonymity.

After everyone dispersed following the festivities, the Maharsha requested that the *Gabbai* disclose to him the identity of this anonymous benefactor. The man was summoned to the Maharsha, who, upon meeting him, realized that he was not a person of great means. He was, therefore, even more curious as to why he had pledged such a large sum. The man

_____

Rabbi Elefant is Executive Rabbinic Coordinator, Kashrus Divison of the Orthodox Union.

informed the Maharsha that, unfortunately, he was childless and was hoping that in the merit of this *mitzvah,* he would be blessed with offspring. The Maharsha immediately blessed him that he should have a son who would study in this very yeshiva.

Not long after, the blessing was fulfilled and a son was born to this childless couple. After the Bar Mitzvah of the boy his father brought him to the yeshiva. As he was yet young, the administrators refused to admit him. Not relenting, the boy's father approached the Maharsha reminding him of his blessing and his commitment. Immediately, the lad was accepted.

Actually, the Talmud in *Moed Katan* indicates that, at the inauguration of the Temple, every attendee's wife conceived a male fetus, for the purpose of the Temple is to serve as a dwelling for the Divine Presence. However, the real place of G-d's dwelling is in Jewish children who are raised with Torah values.

The *Alshich* explains the *pasuk* in *Parshas Terumah,* ועשו לי מקדש ושכנתי בתוכם — "They shall make a Sanctuary for Me so that I may dwell among them" (*Shemos* 25:8). The verse emphasizes that G-d does not really dwell in the Temple, rather He dwells amongst those who open their hearts to Him. Therefore, as the people toiled with such great effort to build a Sanctuary, their reward was to merit righteous children, who would be the real dwelling places of G-d in this world.

A *Bris Milah* marks the starting point of the Jewish child on the road to becoming a fitting abode for the *Shechinah.*

In our *Parshah* the same lesson is taught: כל איש ואשה אשר נדב לבם אתם להביא לכל המלאכה אשר צוה ה' לעשות ביד משה הביאו בני ישראל נדבה לה' —"Every man and woman whose heart moved them to bring for any work that Hashem had commanded to make, through the hands of Moses, the Children of Israel brought a free willed offering to Hashem" (35:29). Explains the *Kehilas Yitzchak,* the Torah is teaching us that, in the merit of their magnanimous gifts and selfless devotion to building the Sanctuary, they were worthy to have righteous "children" who are the real dwelling places of Hashem. However, raising righteous children is an enormous responsibility, which is not achieved easily.

The Torah, in our *Sidrah,* says, ויבאו כל איש אשר נשאו לבו וכל אשר נדבה רוחו אתו הביאו את תרומת ה' למלאכת אהל מועד ולכל עבדתו ולבגדי הקדש — "Every man whose heart inspired him came, and everyone whose generous spirit moved him, brought the portion of Hashem for the work of the Tent of Meeting, for all its labor and for the sacred garments"(35:21).

The Ramban, as expounded by Rabbi Yeruchem Levovitz, zt"l, the famed *Mashgiach* of the Mirrer Yeshiva, explains: "The builders of the Sanctuary are not described by the Torah as the great artisans and architects of their day. Rather, those who demonstrated the greatest devotion to the cause were appointed to build the Temple."

The wisest of all men, Shlomo, teaches us in *Mishlei* (6:6), לך אל נמלה עצל ראה דרכיה וחכם — "Go to the ant, you sluggard, see her ways and grow wise." The commentators explain that the life span of an ant is very short, yet it is very diligent in preparing sustenance that it will probably never use. How much more so is it our obligation to continuously amass merits. Those who possess the quality of constant devotion and diligence are able to rise to the occasion and become the leaders of *Klal Yisrael*.

The Torah tell us, ויצאו כל עדת בני ישראל מלפני משה — "The entire assembly of the Children of Israel left Moses' presence" (35:20). Explains Rav Eliyah Lopian zt"l, that it was noticeable that these people had been in the presence of Moshe. A child raised with the proper values, certainly with a teacher such as Moshe, is forever identifiable. As the Talmud in Tractate *Yoma* (86a) expounds the *pasuk* ואהבת את ה' אלקיך, "You shall love Hashem, your G-d" — act in a way that G-d's Name becomes beloved through you. If one studies in Yeshiva, and then acts properly, people proclaim, "Worthy are his parents who taught him Torah. Worthy are his teachers. How unfortunate are those who did not have such opportunities. How wonderful and fortunate are those who learn Torah."

May the parents of _____ be *zocheh* to raise their son to a life of Torah and *Mitzvos* and be worthy of having him recognized as a true *ben Torah.*

פרשת פקודי
Parshas Pekudei

_____ *Rabbi Abraham D. Mandelbaum*

I N THIS WEEK'S TORAH READING, MOSHE *RABBEINU* IS PRIVILEGED TO SEE THE *Mishkan* completed and all the work performed according to G-d's command. Moshe then blessed the Nation of Israel but the nature of this *berachah* is not revealed. Rashi provides the essence of this blessing: יהי רצון שתשרה שכינה במעשה ידיכם — "Moshe said to them, 'May it be the will of the Almighty that the Divine Presence reside in the works of your hands' " (*Shemos* 39:43).

I would venture to say that anyone who has ever attend a *Bris* would testify that the aforementioned *berachah* is also most appropriate for an eight-day-old infant. There can be no greater blessing than to wish him that G-d's presence always be with him in all his future endeavors — be it Torah, marriage or good deeds.

The story is told of a Jew living in Moscow, just before the disintegration of the Soviet Union, who wanted a *Bris Milah* for his newborn son. Surreptitiously, he summoned a *mohel* to come to his home and perform the ritual circumcision.

As is customary after the *Bris* is completed, the few people who witnessed the religious ceremony, proudly, but quietly, proclaimed כשם שנכנס לברית כן יכנס לתורה ולחפה ולמעשים טובים — "Just as he has entered the covenant so may he enter into Torah, the marriage canopy and good deeds."

The father of the circumcised child indignantly shouted and remon-

_____

Rabbi Mandelbaum is founding rabbi of Ahavat Yisrael in Hewlett, New York

strated the participants by saying "no-no" to this blessing. To the amaze-
ment of those few assembled, he proceeded to explain his sudden out-
burst. He countered that this blessing is inappropriate for his newborn son,
since the plain meaning of the blessing possibly suggests that the *same*
conditions that prevailed at the *Bris* should prevail at the time of his son's
entrance to the study of Torah, his nuptials, and his performance of
mitzvos. Said the father correctly, "I do not wish that communism, despo-
tism, and tyranny be around as my son grows up and becomes involved in
Torah, *Chuppah,* and *Mitzvos.* I hope and pray that by the time he is ready
to enter these religious milestones, he will be living in a free Jewish society
where the practice of Torah and *Mitzvos* will be easily accessible and
encouraged; where freedom of religion will be a right to exercise and
cherish; where being a Torah Jew will be a privilege and a pleasure."

I do not know where this little boy is today, but one thing I know is
that wherever he is, be it in Moscow, Israel or in America, this young
boy is free to practice Torah Judaism and his father's prayer did indeed
come true.

The foremost lesson that we may glean from this story is that we who are
living in these blessed United Sates should not take our freedom of religion for granted. Torah Judaism has made enormous strides in the last 50
years but only because we are privileged to live in a great country where
freedom, and human rights are cherished, preserved and protected. In this
great country of ours, *Yiddishkeit* has flourished beyond our expectations.

Fifty years ago, our detractors, the prophets of doom, predicted that
Orthodoxy was a *negah* (נגע) — a plague in our houses. Fifty years later, we
have demonstrated that Orthodoxy can indeed be an *oneg* (ענג), a true joy
and delight for American Jewry. True, Orthodoxy has invested an inordi-
nate amount of time, effort and money in making Torah Judaism a source
of *nachas* and pride, but only because the climate in our great United
States was fertile and allowed us to sow the seeds of Torah and *Mitzvos.*

The special prayer of כשם שנכנס which the guests respond aloud after
the *Bris* is a most beautiful and wishful prayer, hoping that just as this boy
had the privilege and honor of entering the covenant of Abraham, so may
he also be privileged to enter into Torah study, into marriage and into the
performance of good deeds.

On a more profound level, one discovers that this prayer has a most
magnificent lesson to impart. Hidden beneath the surface is the secret
for Jewish survival and meaningful Jewish living. Torah, marriage and

ethical living require pain, suffering and sacrifice. The message of this prayer is that just as pain and suffering are indispensable to the ritual of circumcision, so too, are they indispensable ingredients in our study of Torah, in our marriage relationship and in our moral and ethical behavior.

Torah study is only acquired through much intellectual rigor and effort. It is not easily gained through osmosis, but only through great endurance, frustration and sacrifice.

The rise in divorce is partially due to the fact that young people do not realize that marriage too requires great effort, endurance, pain, frustrations and sacrifice. The road to a successful marriage is not paved with only bliss and beauty. It requires hard and sometimes painful toil, trials and tribulation. Much sacrifice and compromise are needed to make a marriage work.

Our ability to make moral decisions and behave ethically, which are unique features of our humanity, are based on much spiritual torment, emotional pain, and sacrifice. To live a moral and ethical life is by no means an easy task. It requires enormous moral rectitude, and spiritual courage to resist and overcome the blandishments of greed, pleasure, and self-gratification. Here too, a Torah Jew needs to realize the great effort, commitment and personal sacrifice one has to experience in order to achieve a life of *maasim tovim*, good deeds.

May the parents of this infant be blessed with the wisdom and ability to impart the three aspects of the בשם *berachah* and raise him to be a true *ben Torah*. We wish you much *nachas*, happiness, and success.
Mazel Tov.

~§ Sefer Vayikra

פרשת ויקרא
Parshas Vayikra

_____ *Rabbi Morey Schwartz*

THE OCCASION OF A *BRIS* LEAVES US ALL WONDERING WHAT TO THINK, WHAT TO feel. Of course the birth of a new human being is a time of great celebration, of uncontainable joy; still, we must wonder as we witness this mysterious tradition of our people, what is its meaning, what is its significance? And why are we all here to experience it . . . what message does it convey?

The word, *Bris,* or covenant, is an essential concept to our people. Without it, we would not understand our role in the world. We would not have the faith to believe that we would survive all that the world has sent our way. The *Bris Milah* has been the key to our survival. But even more, this eternal covenant, which we perpetuate here today, is an ongoing reminder of the way we look at the world around us.

In *Parshas Vayirka,* the Torah instructs us in the fine details of *Korbanos.* There the Torah refers to another *bris,* one not made directly with man, but seemingly, made with salt: וכל קרבן מנחתך במלח תמלח ולא תשבית מלח ברית מלח — "And every meal offering you shall season with salt; you shall not withhold the salt of the Covenant of your G-d from your meal offering, with all of your offerings you shall offer salt" (2:13).

Are we to understand that G-d made a covenant with salt (מלח ברית אלקיך)? Rashi quotes the Midrash purporting exactly that to be the case!

_____

Rabbi Schwartz recently made aliyah *to Hashmonaim, Israel and serves as a* Mohel *for the Modiin region.*

During the six days of creation, says the Midrash, G-d made a *bris* with the waters of the deep that salt would be used on every *Korban*. This covenant was made to give the earthly waters (from which salt comes) a share in the *Korbanos* and thereby bring them closer to Hashem. He also promised that the water would be poured during the ceremonies of *nisuch ha'mayim,* water libations.

The Rambam, however, says something more oriented to the *peshat,* the simple meaning. He comments that G-d requested that we enter into a covenant. Hashem asked that we promise never to bring an offering without salt, because such a bland or tasteless offering would be shameful before Him. If it's not tasty enough for humans to delight in, then neither will G-d find satisfaction in such an offering.

Perhaps that lesson is a lesson for **all** covenants made by G-d with mankind, including the covenant of Abraham which we celebrate here today. This is to say, that if the behavior manifested through the upholding of a covenant is not suitable to be admired and celebrated by mankind — like an unseasoned piece of meat — then similarly, it is a *bizayon,* it is shameful and undesirable before G-d.

As we pray that this child live a life of Torah, we also pray that the Torah he lives and breathes be a source of delight to all who know him.

As we pray that this child be blessed to enter the *chuppah,* we also pray that the marriage he commits to shall be a source of celebration for him, his wife, his children, and all who know them.

As we pray that this child be blessed to live a life filled with acts of kindness, we also pray that all of his actions will be admired by all who have contact with him. May his service of G-d not only be exacting, but may it be in good taste as well.

פרשת צו
Parshas Tzav

_____ *Rabbi Mordecai H. Feuerstein*

THE PROCEDURES WITH WHICH THE *KOHANIM* INAUGURATED EACH NEW DAY IN the *Beis Hamikdash,* described at the beginning of *Parshas Tzav,* reflect concepts worthy of consideration at the inauguration of an infant into the *Bris* of Avraham *Avinu.*

The Temple day began with a two-fold service (*Avodah*). The first one was תרומת הדשן, lifting up a portion of the previous day's ashes from the altar. The *kohen* scooped up a shovelful from the innermost ashes on the "large pyre" (מערכה גדולה) atop the altar — from the burnt flesh of the previous day's offerings (especially the *olah,* which was the last offering of the previous day) — descended with it to the floor of the Courtyard, and placed it alongside the eastern base of the altar, in a designated place (מקום הדשן).

תרומת הדשן was followed by הוצאת הדשן which involved removing and cleaning excess ashes from the altar. This pragmatic procedure enabled the fires on top of the altar to burn more effectively and efficiently.

Three principles in *Avodas Hashem* can be gleaned from תרומת הדשן (lifting up the ashes) and הוצאת הדשן (removing the ashes).

Rabbi Samson Raphael Hirsch explains that the act of תרומת הדשן is *not* part of the preparation of the altar for the *avodah* of the new day which is about to begin. At the crack of dawn, after the *kohen* donned the priestly

_____
Rabbi Feuerstein is rabbi of the Synagogue of the Suburban Torah Center, Livingston, New Jersey.

garments, the first thing he did was to lift a handful of the ashes from the *olah*-offering of the day before and place it beside the altar as an *azkarah,* a remembrance, of the previous day's sacrifices. Thus, תרומת הדשן should be seen as the conclusion of the *Avodah* of the preceding day. Only then does the preparation of the altar for the new day commence with הוצאת הדשן, removing excess ashes to facilitate the effectiveness of the pyres (מערכות). The message according to Rav Hirsch is as follows: *Today* does not brings a new mission. It is a continuation, to carry out the mission that yesterday was to accomplish, the very obligations that our ancestors bore. Each new day adds its contribution to the fulfillment of the one task assigned to all generations of the House of Israel. The Jewish "today" has to take its mission from its "yesterday." Therefore, תרומת הדשן is a re-minder of the permanence of that which was dedicated and sacrificed to G-d on the previous day.

The הוצאת הדשן, on the other hand, expresses the contrasting thought — that every new day presents a challenge to accomplish the whole Jewish mission afresh. Woe unto him who with smug complacency thinks he can rest on his laurels, on what he has already achieved, and who does not meet the task of each new day with full devotion as if it were the first day of his life's work! הוציא את הדשן — every trace of yesterday's sacrifice is to be removed so that the service of the new day can be started on a completely fresh basis. The past remains and should not be forgotten (symbolized by the תרומת הדשן), but it should be retired to the background (taken down to the floor of the Courtyard).

The *mitzvah* of תרומת הדשן and the instructions regarding הוצאת הדשן are the first commands in *Sefer Vayikra* addressed *directly* to Aharon. Until this point, all of the instructions that G-d gave are given to *b'nei Aharon,* the sons of Aharon, never to Aharon, himself. Midrash Rabbah tells us that Moshe had become alarmed about this seemingly exclusionary pat-tern. He wondered: perhaps G-d is angry with Aharon. G-d responded that, to prove this was not the case, He would bestow a *mitzvah* directly on Aharon, which would reflect His special love for Aharon. Hence, *Parshas Tzav* begins: "Hashem spoke to Moshe saying: Command Aharon and his sons . . ." (*Vayikra* 6:1-2).

Rabbi Mordechai Miller (*Sabbath Shiurim,* vol. I) asks the obvious ques-tion: Lifting up and clearing out the ashes would seem to be a menial job. How does it show G-d's special love and esteem for Aharon?

Rabbi Miller directs our attention to the answer of the *Chasam Sofer* who cites the classic work, *Chovas HaLevavos* (11th century), which states (*Sha'ar Hak'ni'ah,* Chapt 6, par 7): "When performing an act for the sake of G-d, one should forget his own importance, honor, and dignity, whether he is alone or in the midst of assemblies. We learn this from Aharon — in spite of the high dignity of his office: 'He shall remove the ashes' — Hashem obligated him to remove the ashes daily, to induce humility and remove arrogance from his heart."

In all other practical *mitzvos* of the priesthood, Aharon's sons could effectively replace him. Therefore, so as not to burden Aharon, the directives regarding various sacrifices and procedures were given to them. But in this one *mitzvah,* of removing the ashes, he was irreplaceable precisely because of his greatness, and the point could be perfectly illustrated.

Thus, הרמת והוצאת הדשן teaches us the need to be humble in our service of Hashem, suffused with a sense of the great privilege we have to fulfill His word, no matter how menial the task may seem.

Although תרומת הדשן is counted as one of the 613 *mitzvos,* הוצאת הדשן is not. Rather, its performance facilitates the *avodah* (מכשירי עבודה). That is why no lottery was held among the *kohanim* for the privilege of performing it.

Nevertheless, the Mishnah (*Tamid* 2:2) says: מימיו לא נתעצל הכהן מלהוציא את הדשן — "Never was the *kohen* lax about taking out the ashes." Even though הוצאת הדשן did not have the status of other *avodah* performances, since it beautified the altar and enabled it to function more efficiently, the *kohen* was never reluctant to do it. On the contrary, he considered it a privilege and volunteered to do it with enthusiasm.

The unflagging commitment of the *kohen* in "clearing out the ashes" exemplifies the importance of זריזות (eagerness and alacrity) and התלהבות (a sense of excitement and enthusiasm) in carrying out not only *mitzvos*, but all activities which are necessary for *halachic* requirements to be met.

These lessons — carrying forward the mission of the past through our new and creative efforts today, and the need for humble submission and enthusiasm in the service of G-d — are reflected in the *mitzvah* of *Bris Milah.*

Bris Milah is counted among the ten trials Abraham faced, not only because of the danger of this unprecedented procedure but because it threatened to seriously contradict his lifelong method of bringing people close to G-d. Abraham was worried that it would be regarded as bizarre by the public and cause people to shun him (*Michtav M'Eliyahu*). He did not want to lose his connection with the mission of yesterday — calling and attracting people בשם ה' — as a result of the *avodah* which was being demanded of him today. Nevertheless, in a display of זריזות and התלהבות, he humbly submitted to the will of G-d, on the very day the *mitzvah* was promulgated (*Ramban, Sefer Bereishis* 17:26).

On celebrating this occasion, as we come to inaugurate the רך הנמול into the *Bris* of Avraham *Avinu*, we pray that the principles gleaned from the daily inaugural procedures of the *Kohanim* in the *Beis HaMikdash* be realized in his life, and that he grow to be a source of pride to his family. May they merit to raise him לתורה ולחפה ולמעשים טובים.

פרשת שמיני
Parshas Shemini

James Di Poce, M.D.

A T FIRST GLANCE, ONE MIGHT WONDER WHY _PARSHAS SHEMINI_ BEGINS "AND it was on the eighth day that Moshe called to Aharon and his sons, and the elders of Israel [to begin serving in the _Mishkan_]" as, in fact, it was the first day of the official operation of the _Mishkan_ and might appropriately be called the "first day." The _Rishonim_ state that this was actually the eighth day of preparation for the inauguration of the _Mishkan_. The question remains, however, why is this day referred to as number eight and not number one? Perhaps we can suggest one answer which relates to the nature of the seven preceding days of inauguration. The _Rishonim_ state that these were days when Moshe _Rabbeinu,_ himself, performed the service in the _Mishkan_ in order to teach the _Kohanim._ This concept — not defining the first day of official operation as day one, but rather day eight — shows the importance of preparation before beginning any endeavor. Similarly, the birth of a child does not mark the beginning of its educational life, but rather, the birth was preceded by years of preparation.

The _Kli Yakar_ is likewise bothered by the significance of the fact that the official opening of the _Mishkan_ occurred on the "eighth day." He states that the number eight represents transcending nature. For this reason says the _Kli Yakar, Bris Milah_ occurs on day eight, and furthermore this is why _Milah_ on day number eight sets aside the laws of Shabbos which occurs each week on the seventh day. The _Kli Yakar_ supports his contention from a midrash in _Yalkut Shimoni_ (# 241) which refers to the number eight as

---

Dr. Di Poce in a resident in radiology at Jacobi Hospital, Bronx, New York.

being supernatural. The midrash notes that Moshe and the *Bnei Yisrael* sang אז ישיר and the numerical value of אז is eight. Taken in the context of the fact that there was a tremendous revelation of Hashem's presence at the splitting of the *Yam Suf*, to the extent that even a maidservant had the level of prophecy of Yechezkel, this supernatural state and its relationship to the number eight is apparent.

In this framework, what then is the significance of the number eight and *Bris Milah*? It would seem that *Bris Milah*, which brings a baby into the fold of *Yehadus*, establishes a supernatural bond with Hashem through His covenant. This bond ensures that we are not merely governed indirectly by Hashem through the laws of nature, but rather that our lives are *directly* influenced by *Hashgacha Pratis* (Divine Providence).

This aspect of *Bris Milah* becomes apparent through another set of *midrashim* about the *galus Mitzrayim* which is connected to the third verse in *Parshas Shemini*. The verse states that two of the first sacrifices brought in the *Mishkan* were an עגל (a calf) and a שעיר עזים (a goat). The *Chizkuni* points out a *Sifra* stating that the calf served to atone for the sin of the Golden Calf, whereas the goat served to atone for the sale of Yosef (since his brothers slaughtered a goat to dip Yosef's coat in its blood to deceive their father Yaakov). *Pirkei d'Rebbi Eliezer* notes that the *Bnei Yisrael* merited redemption from *Mitzrayim* because they did not change their names, language, or dress. Yet another midrash states that it was the blood of *Milah* and the blood of the *Pesach* sacrifice that merited redemption for *Bnei Yisroel.* What is the significance of both of these *midrashim*? It would seem that maintaining their language, names, and dress distinguished the *Bnei Yisroel* from their neighbors, the *Mitzrim,* for the entire duration of their stay in *Mitzrayim.* Moreover, it is these three things which distinguish any nation from another. Had the *Bnei Yisrael* not maintained these three characteristics, it seems reasonable to assume that they would have completely assimilated to the extent that there would not have been a nation to redeem. Once the *Bnei Yisrael* were able to maintain themselves as a nation, they demonstrated that they were not only a nation, but a nation that set aside idolatry as represented by the *Pesach* sacrifice, and a nation which is truly an *Am Kadosh* (a holy nation) as represented by their supernatural bond to Hashem through *Bris Milah*. Nevertheless, what is the significance of the need to atone for the sale of Yosef at the opening ceremony of the *Mishkan*? It would seem that the sale of Yosef set the stage for a family of 70 to go down to *Mitzrayim* and to emerge as a nation of more than 600,000. Hence, the chapter of the birth of a nation which began with *mechiras* Yosef is brought to closure with the inception of the *Mishkan,* the place of the most intimate revelation of Hashem to the *Bnei Yisrael.* The *Mishkan* and its travels, therefore, marks the next period in the history of *Yehadus,* a history that each and every Jew is connected to by the supernatural bond of *Bris Milah.*

May the parents instill the lessons of *Parshas Shemini* in their new son — to prepare well before beginning an endeavor and to govern his life based on the special bond with Hashem first established today at his *Bris Milah* — recognizing the element of *Hoshgacha Pratis* in our lives. In this way they will raise him to a life of Torah and *maasim tovim.*

פרשת תזריע
Parshas Tazria

_____ *Rabbi Elazar Lew*

"ON THE EIGHTH DAY, THE FLESH OF HIS FORESKIN SHALL BE CIRCUMCISED" (*Vayikra* 12:3). Although the commandment of circumcision had already been given to Avraham, it is repeated here. *Bris Milah,* as enumerated in *Minchas Chinuch,* is the second *mitzvah* in the Torah. But, like the *mitzvah* of פרו ורבו, the first *mitzvah* in the Torah, and the *mitzvah* of גיד הנשה, the third *mitzvah, Bris Milah* when commanded to Avraham, was given before *Matan Torah,* the Revelation at Mount Sinai. The commandment of circumcision is repeated here to teach us two new laws from the above quoted verse. Since the Torah states, וביום השמיני, "on the eighth day" we learn that *Milah* may be performed ONLY in the daytime (from the word ביום meaning "day"). Also, as the Talmud teaches us (*Shabbos* 132), the Torah says, "On the eighth day" to teach us that a child MUST be circumcised on the eighth day after his birth, even if it falls on the Sabbath, unless of course, the infant's health requires a delay.

The question that still remains is why does the commandment of *Milah* appear HERE — in the midst of a passage about the laws of ritual contamination and purity?

Rabbi Zalman Sorotzkin explains that just as the Torah gave two signs to distinguish the pure from the impure among animals (split hooves and chewing the cud) and fish (fins and scales), the Torah also gives two signs to distinguish the most excellent type of human being. The two signs,

_____

Rabbi Lew is a member of the Kashrus division of the Orthodox Union.

90 ⤳ ENTERING THE COVENANT

circumcision and immersion in the *mikvah,* identify the man who belongs to "a kingdom of priests and a holy nation" (*Shemos* 19:6). At Mount Sinai, before Hashem could make a covenant with our forefathers and give them the Torah, they had to undergo circumcision and immersion (*Kerisos* 9). Similarly, a non-Jew who wishes to join the holy nation does not become a convert until he has undergone circumcision and immersion (*Yevamos* 46).

This rule applies to those who were not born holy. But for those who were born holy — whose parents were already included in the covenant — one of the two signs (immersion) must precede their conception. In other words, the mother must observe the laws of *Niddah,* menstrual separation and then purification through immersion in the *mikvah* — "as during the days of her separation (*niddah*) infirmity shall she be contaminated" (*Vayikra* 12:2). Afterwards, when the offspring is born in purity, our verse states: "On the eighth day, the flesh of his foreskin shall be circumcised."

Shlomo *HaMelech* joined these two commandments together as well, when he said, "Give a portion to seven and also to eight" (*Koheles* 11:2). "Give a portion to seven" — these are the seven days of *niddah.* "And also to eight" — these are the eight days of circumcision. Hashem says, "If you observe the days of *niddah* I will give you a son, and you will circumcise him on the eighth day." That is why it says: "On the eighth day, the flesh of his foreskin shall be circumcised."

Now we may better understand the sequence of the Torah sections. As R' Shamlai stated: The law for the human being is placed after the law for all other living creatures (see Rashi to *Vayikra* 12:2 at the beginning of the *Parshah*). After setting forth "the law of the animal, the bird, every living creature" (*Vayikra* 11:46), the Torah continues with the law of that human being who is worthy of being called "man," and the "two signs of purity" which distinguish him.

Circumcision is associated with Eliyahu *HaNavai.* We have a custom of setting aside a handsome chair as the "Throne of Eliyahu." Our Rabbis instituted the ritual of placing the infant on the Throne of Eliyahu during the circumcision, since Eliyahu attends every *Bris.* After the infant is placed upon the Throne of Eliyahu, the *Mohel* makes the statement: אליהו מלאך הברית — "Eliyahu the messenger of the covenant." The term מלאך הברית is found in *Malachi 3:1* where Radak refers it to Eliyahu *HaNavi,* who will come to herald the Redemption. In the merit of our performing the *mitzvah* of *Milah,* may we all be worthy of seeing Eliyahu *HaNavi* come to herald the *Moshiach* speedily in our day.

פרשת מצורע
Parshas Metzora

— for a *Pidyon Haben*

_____ *Rabbi Yosef Grossman*

A T FIRST GLANCE IT APPEARS THAT THERE IS NOTHING TO LINK THE JOY OF *Pidyon Haben* with the gloom of *tzaraas.* There seems to be no connection between the emotional ecstasy of the father's recitation of the *Shehecheyanu* blessing at the *Pidyon Haben* and the tears welling in the homeowner's eyes as he watches his *tzaraas* afflicted house being demolished in front of him. A closer and deeper analysis, however, reveals an underlying philosophy and *Hashkafah* which unites these two precepts into one entity.

Let us begin with *tzaraas.* Rambam (*Hilchos Tumas Tzaraas* 16:10) sees these supernatural afflictions as Divine punishment for selfish behavior and gossip. Concerning נגעי בתים, the *tzaraas* of houses, Rambam adds that Hashem mercifully begins by afflicting property, before striking the person's body.

The Talmud (*Yoma* 11b) derives the above mentioned selfish demeanor leading to *tzaraas* from *Vayikra* 14:35 which describes the owner of the house as אשר לו הבית — "the one to whom the house belongs." It is **his house** and no one else's!

Tzror Hamor adds a penetrating insight. The homeowner felt that the house is exclusively his and he need not share his blessings with anyone else. But the Almighty Who gave him what he has, wants him to share with others. G-d can easily give man more or take away what he is misusing due

_____

Rabbi Grossman is rabbinic coordinator, Kashrus division of the Orthodox Union.

to selfish behavior.

Let us now direct our attention to the *mitzvah* of *Pidyon Haben*. According to Rav Samson Raphael Hirsch, *zt'l* (*Shemos* 13:13) the three categories of the sanctification of the firstborn i.e. בכור בהמה טהורה, בכור אדם and פטר חמור represents Man (אדם), his food (בהמה טהורה) and his possessions (חמור). Thus, the sanctification of the firstborn declares that (1) the family, (2) the food of the family, and (3) their possessions *all* belong to Hashem.

But what of the individual who imagines that he will increase his property by withholding his possessions from holiness and sanctification? What if he will not redeem that which G-d obligates him to redeem? He will find, continues Rav Hirsch (ibid), "that he has fallen into a grave error. ואם לא תפדה וערפתו — "if you do not redeem it, you shall axe the back of its neck" is inscribed over every Jewish fortune. He who selfishly intends to keep everything for himself, is himself sentencing it to destruction." Thus, according to Rav Hirsch, not only "**must** you kill the firstborn donkey by breaking its neck" but you **are,** in fact, **sentencing** it to its ultimate Divine decreed destruction if you fail to redeem it.

The lesson of *tzaraas* is thus connected with that of *Pidyon Haben*. The "his house" philosophy must be replaced with a capital H — His house *Hashkafah*. It is **not** your house — it is His house. It is **not** your child — it is G-d's child. All that you, man, have and possess — your wife — your child — your home — your food — your every breath — life itself — it is not yours — it is Hashem's. It is holy and sanctified and must be used as G-d dictates and shared with others.

The contemporary Jew would do well to internalize this common *Pidyon Haben-Tzaraas* message. Then — and only then — will he be able to adequately deliver a response to that question asked by his child in the verse which immediately follows the *mitzvah* of *Pidyon Haben*.

"And it will be when your son asks you in time to come saying, 'What is this?' that you will say to him. 'By strength of hand did Hashem bring us out from Egypt, out of the house of bondage' " (*Shemos* 13:14).

Realizing that the entire Universe is Hashem's, helps us to understand that He is the Master of time as well. It is His strong hand that led the enslaved Jews out of Egypt and continues to lead our people throughout the millennia.

The father who joyfully declares the שהחייינו *berachah* at his son's *Pidyon Haben* is, in fact, declaring that time (לזמן הזה) and his family — his son —

all belong to Hashem — everything is His. He reaffirms his complete rejection of the "his house" philosophy. This philosophy also, unfortunately, leads to history becoming "his story" devoid of Divine intervention. At the same time, the new father boldly declares that Hashem is both Master of the Universe and of His(s)tory as well.

פרשת אחרי מות
Parshas Acharei Mos

_____ *Rabbi Menachem Genack*

W HEN AHARON *HAKOHEN* ENTERED THE HOLY OF HOLIES ON YOM KIPPUR HE entered, in the words of the Midrash (*Yalkut Shimoni, Parshas Acharei Mos*), with "a bundle of *mitzvos* in hand." One of them, the Midrash goes on to say, was the *mitzvah* of *Milah*. The Midrash interprets the verse describing Aharon's entrance to the Holy of Holies, בזאת יבא אהרן אל הקדש — "With *this* (זאת) Aharon entered. . ." (*Vayikra* 16:3) to be a reference to the verse in *Bereishis* where G-d instructs Avraham about the *mitzvah* of *Milah*, "This (זאת) is the *Bris* you shall guard" (*Bereishis* 17: 10).

The connection between the *Kohen Gadol* in the Holy of Holies and the *Bris* of Avraham *Avinu* is a profound one. On Yom Kippur the *Kohen Gadol* stood alone in front of G-d. His solitude was all the more dramatic in the Holy of Holies, a place that was separate, pristine, and dark. The *mitzvah* of *Milah* also bears a quality of being separate and alone. It is, more than any other *mitzvah*, associated with Avraham *Avinu*, who is depicted in the Torah as a man isolated and lonely.

Avraham proclaims G-d and a new monotheistic theology in a world that had completely forgotten Him. That expression of total loneliness comes to its peak at the *Akeidah*, the binding of Isaac. Indeed, the word Hebrew, *Ivri*, according to the Rabbis, means "opposite shore"; for Avraham was on one shore and the entire world was on the opposite shore. This could have precipitated in Avraham a sense of isolation, frustration, bitterness and

_____

Rabbi Genack is rabbinic administrator of the Orthodox Union's Kashrus division and rav of Congregation Shomrei Emunah in Englewood, New Jersey.

misanthropy. But he remained the paradigm of kindness, hospitality, love and concern — even for the iniquitous cities of Sodom and Gomorrah.

The *Milah* distinguished Avraham as a man of G-d. But distinction is, perforce, separation. The *Milah,* as much as it was a recognition of Avraham's unique status, also distanced him from the rest of mankind.

The father, by bringing his son to *Bris Milah,* endows him with the quality of Avraham *Avinu,* the lonely knight of faith, and thereby affirms the principles of Torah. This struggle, which is the destiny of every Jew, is a lonely but heroic one. The רך הנמול should merit to see worlds of spirituality that no one has yet merited to see. May his parents and entire family have much *nachas* from him.

פרשת קדשים
Parshas Kedoshim

_____ Ari Dov Ganchrow

THE CUSTOM DURING A *BRIS MILAH* IS THAT AS THE *MOHEL* PERFORMS THE circumcision the father makes the following *Berachah*: להכניסו בבריתו של אברהם אבינו — "to enter him into the covenant of Abraham our forefa-ther." At this point the congregation respond, כשם שנכנס לברית כן יכנס לתורה ולחפה ולמעשים טובים — "just as he entered into the covenant so may he enter into the Torah, the marriage canopy and good deeds." Subse-quently, the baby is given a name and the congregation repeats the bless-ing of כשם a second time.

Why is this blessing repeated? And, furthermore, why of all the mile-stones that a child will face over a lifetime have our rabbis chosen to mention Torah, *Chuppah,* and *Maasim Tovim*?

The Midrash in *Parshas Kedoshim* is extremely instructive in this regard. The *pasuk* states: וכי תבאו אל הארץ ונטעתם כל עץ מאכל וערלתם ערלתו את פריו שלש שנים יהיה לכם ערלים לא יאכל — "When you shall come to the land and you shall plant any food tree you shall treat its fruit as forbidden. For three years they shall be forbidden to you, they shall not be eaten" (*Vayikra* 19:23).

Although the simple explanation deals with agricultural laws the Midrash (Chapter 35 verse 6) says: "Rabbi Akivah says there are four kinds of *Orlah,* and this expression describes the imperfections of the ear, the mouth, the heart, and the body."

In the time of the Prophets, the term ערל, "uncircumcised" was applied

_____
Mr. Ganchrow is an attorney living in Teaneck, New Jersey.

allegorically to the rebellious heart or the obdurate ear. The word ערל describes the lips of a person whose speech is not fluent, or the heart and ear of a person who will not listen to reason.

The Midrash continues: "On which organ are we commanded to perform circumcision? If man should perform it on the ear he would no longer be without blemish. Likewise, should he perform it on the mouth he would also not be without blemish. Says Rabbi Akivah, "At what spot should we perform circumcision and remain without blemish? It is only the ערלה pertaining to the membrum verile.

I heard from my Rebbe, Harav Meir Golvicht, that these four *orlos* (coverings) of the ear, mouth, heart and the body represent the source of life for the Jewish people. The ערלת המילה, penile membrane, represents the future of the Jewish family. It is the covenant that guarantees continuity from Abraham to the present and future generations. The ערלת הפה, the oral orifice, represents the building of personality, communication, and interacting with society and our fellow Jews. This can only come about when we understand one another through the power of speech. So great is the power of the spoken word that the Talmud tells us, כל המלמד בן חברו תורה כאלו ילדו — "One who teaches his friend's son Torah it is as though he gave birth to him." The ערלת הלב, covering of the heart represents the source of life. King Solomon teaches us in *Mishlei*, מכל משמר נצר לבך כי ממנו תוצאות חיים — "More than you guard anything guard your heart, for from it are the sources of life . . ." (*Mishlei* 4:23). It is important in life to be calm, relaxed and compassionate and not take everything to heart.

The last *orlah* is ערלת אזנים, the covering of the ears. The ears represent the ability to listen and absorb information. There are great benefits to be had if we only realize that there are many individuals we will encounter who possess much knowledge and are willing to share it with each of us.

The *Bris Milah* is a step in the perfection of the Jewish personality. At first we remove the physical *orlah*, which constitutes the act of *Bris Milah*. The joy that is shared by the family and friends is manifest by the manifold blessings of Torah, *Chuppah*, and *Maasim Tovim*. The *Bris Milah* is but the first step. One must learn and come to the realization that a Jew's responsibility lies in three different spheres — בין אדם למקום, בין אדם לחברו, ובין אדם לעצמו — his relationship to G-d, to man and himself. Failing to appreciate these responsibilities would forever freeze the individual in an infantile state. Unlike the sons of Ishmael who performed circumcision as an end in itself, the Jew is given a name by his parents and now we must contemplate the life that lies ahead that will require the assistance of family, friends, teachers and most of all the blessings of Hashem. Thus, once the child's identity is clearly established we again bless the child with כשם שנכנס לברית כן יכנס לתורה ולחפה ולמעשים טובים — Just as the child entered the covenant of Abraham without any ulterior motive, so too, shall he be blessed to go through the stages of life, as a *talmid chacham, chassan,* and a performer of *mitzvos,* with total piety.

Each character trait requires perfection. The ערלת פה can be developed by learning and speaking the words of Torah. ערלת אזנים represents the *Chuppah* because the source of a caring household is when a husband and wife can listen to each other and be true partners. And ערלת הלב represents מעשים טובים, good deeds — compassion for our fellow human beings regardless of who they are.

The *Bris Milah* is only the first stage of Jewish life as represented by the ערלת המילה. Our hope and prayer is that over the years this child shall develop and conquer all the other *orlos.* May he be a source of pride and joy to his family and *Klal Yisrael.*

פרשת אמור
Parshas Emor

Rabbi Mark Nenner

TODAY, THERE IS, PERHAPS, NO QUALITY SOUGHT OUT MORE BY MODERN MAN, than spirituality. The ability to find meaning in ordinary life is a pursuit that is sweeping our nation. From the widespread study of _Kabbala,_ to the Dali Lama, our society is preoccupied with this quest. But what is Judaism's view? What does the Almighty have to say about the definition of holiness?

The Torah tells us in _Parshas Emor,_ that the _Kohen_ is prohibited from defiling himself by coming into contact with a dead body. Of all the things that come to mind, isn't it strange that the Torah's definition of spiritual purity is contingent upon life and death? Is this the basis on which we judge our closeness to God? Why is there no mention of prayer or Torah study, of sacrifices or fasting? How are we to understand the Torah's directive to the _Kohen_? What is it about the _Kohen_ that requires him to be kept away from the dead? And if there _is_ a concept of טומאת המת (defilement of a deceased), why aren't the rest of the Jewish people given this _mitzvah_? Weren't we _all_ commanded in the previous _parshah_ to be a holy nation?

It is not coincidental that the Jewish view of purity and contamination is a widely misunderstood phenomenon. Indeed, as many outreach professionals will attest to, ours is a system that is often maligned. The word "impure" conjures up images of filth and dirt, and is therefore an area that needs a great deal of explanation. Yet, isn't it interesting, that while we ponder the meanings of these terms, we never stop to question the

Rabbi Nenner is rav of Young Israel of Holliswood, Holliswood, New York.

practice of washing our hands upon leaving the cemetery? Clearly, an explanation is in order. The commentaries explain that there is a unique relationship that exists between the physicality of the body and spirituality of the soul. Each has particular needs that have to be satisfied. What is unique about Jews, however, is that we believe that physical and spiritual pleasure need not be a contradiction. Our mission is to build a relationship with God *through* the physical trappings of this world. This, to many, is a foreign concept. In other faiths, physical pleasure is seen as a weakness of the flesh, and is eliminated as a means of seeking out the holy. One who wishes to achieve this holiness is encouraged to remain celibate, to abstain from earthly pleasures.

But Jews do not subscribe to this philosophy of asceticism. Our job is to live a physical existence, and to inject holiness into our everyday lives. Hearty Shabbos meals, a restful vacation, a long run in the park, all of these are avenues through which we can achieve higher levels of spirituality. The key to this mission is to channel our actions toward the service of Hashem. As we say in the prayer, אנו רצים והם רצים רצים "we run as does the rest of the world," but only *our* efforts are in pursuit of eternity.

With this explanation in mind, we can now address the problem at hand. A body is only considered to be holy, as long as it houses the soul that drives it. As the soul departs, so does the spirituality that accompanies it. What is left is the total physical nature of the body. This absence of spirituality is known as *Tumah.* The *Kohen,* as Rav Moshe Feinstein *zt'l,* explains, was the epitome of holiness. His full-time job was the service of Hashem, and therefore he could not subject himself to defilement by the corporeal body. Ordinary man, who is involved in the more mundane matters of life, has the obligation of tending to the dead.

The opportunity to direct one's actions toward the service of Heaven is what makes our heritage so meaningful. To have purpose in life is a basic, yet often unmet, need of human existence. Without it, life is reduced to a series of trivial and inconsequential events, which span the course of merely a few decades. Man works and struggles; in a short time it is over, and all he is left with is physical and transient. But if we realize that by directing our efforts we can achieve immortality, the effects on our behavior will be remarkable. Such an attitude will make us better sons and daughters, better spouses, better parents, and ultimately, better servants of the Almighty.

The birth of a child, aside from being a momentous occasion, brings with it an awesome amount of responsibility. The decisions we make as parents today, are ones that will shape the course of generations to come. Our job is to ensure that the lives of our offspring are infused with direction and meaning. A *Bris* is the event in which we begin to give life its definition. It is the distinction we give to the most carnal part of the body, which elevates it to the realm of the spiritual.

Dear parents, you have spent your entire lives preparing for this moment. Your devotion and dedication toward the *Ribono Shel Olam* are about to undergo a huge transition. For you no longer function as individuals, but as the matriarch and patriarch of future generations.

May you continue to live your lives with purpose and may your new son be *zocheh* to carry on your legacy and be a great source of pride and *nachas* to you and your entire family. Mazel Tov!

פרשת בהר
Parshas Behar

_____ Rabbi Reuven P. Bulka

COUNTING IS A SIGNIFICANT PART OF THE JEWISH EXPERIENCE. THE COUNTING that stands out most is that which links Pesach to Shavuos. However, there are other countings that form part of our lifestyle, including the woman's counting of the days before going to the *mikvah,* which is certainly a more personal and private count. Then there is the most public daily count leading up to Shabbos at the conclusion of the daily prayers through an appropriate psalm for that day, indicating in the preamble what day it is in the countdown to Shabbos.

There is another count that is of singular importance, but which no longer prevails. This is the counting of the years — seven years, seven times, leading to the *Yovel* year, the fiftieth jubilee year (*Vayikra* 25:8). *Toras Kohanim* indicates that this count is not the responsibility of each individual. It is rather a responsibility, which rests with the Great *Sanhedrin* — the Jewish High Court (*Beis Din HaGadol*).

According to *Aruch HaShulchan,* the High Court would rise on Rosh Hashanah and recite a blessing which reads approximately as follows — *"Blessed are you, Lord our God —Ruler of the universe, Who has sanctified us with the commandments and has commanded us concerning the counting of the Shemitah." Today is the first year for the Shemitah."* On the eighth year, the count would be — *"Today is eight years, which is one whole sabbatical (seven years) and one year towards the Jubilee (fiftieth year)."* And so it would continue, much like the *berachah* for

_____
Rabbi Bulka is rav of Congregation Machzikei Hadas, Ottawa, Ontario, Canada.

the *Omer* that is counted between Pesach and Shavuos.

Why is the count of the years delegated to the Great *Sanhedrin,* whereas the count of the days is given over to all Israel? Perhaps, because the count linking Pesach to Shavuos impresses upon each individual that the celebration of Pesach should lead to a full acceptance of the Torah on Shavuos. It is not merely the community in general that is accepting the Torah, but each and every individual within that community.

However, concerning the jubilee year, there are specific responsibilities in the fiftieth year that may not necessarily apply to every individual. Not everyone has servants that have to be freed; not everyone has land that must be returned; not everyone has land, for which there is a universal prohibition against planting and harvesting.

It, therefore, becomes the obligation of the Great *Sanhedrin* to publicly do the counting. This reminds the people as to what year in the cycle-to-ward-Jubilee they are at present, and thereby enables them to prepare, both generally and specifically, for the fiftieth year.

But there is more that is achieved by mandating that the Great *Sanhedrin* publicly count the years leading up to *Yovel.* The counting creates a focus. At no point should the community go from year to year in a disjointed, incoherent way. Instead, each year must be connected to the next, all gearing towards the climactic moment of the fiftieth year.

That climactic moment is the time when everything returns to the original status quo. The land is left alone so that everyone has equal claim to it. The original division of the land is re-established, and all individuals who are in servitude regain their freedom.

The high court reminds the entire community, through this public counting, that our lives should have a focus. That focal point should always be directed towards expressing human dignity, and the responsibility to share with others. This is the purpose of the count. Through this we will make sure that every action and every person really matters.

The entry into the covenant (*Bris Milah*) and the redemption of the firstborn (*Pidyon Haben*) similarly come after precise counting to the eighth day or the completion of thirty days, respectively. But from that point on, there is no countdown toward Bar Mitzvah. However, it would be a mistake to lose sight of the end goal, what may be considered as a sort of jubilee, or *yovel* — to a completion of a stage in life — for children.

Rather than viewing child-raising on a day-to-day basis only, it is vital that we have a vision of what we want our children to be — Godly-inspired,

Torah-committed, and community-dedicated. To achieve this, we need to count the years, to have an incremental plan for how our children will develop. In short, we must make every day count.

We celebrate this *simcha* with the fervent hope that the visions and aspirations that the parents and community have for this newly covenanted (or redeemed) child will be realized, and that this child will be counted among the valued members of the community.

פרשת בחקתי
Parshas Bechukosai

_____ *Rabbi Moshe Shulman*

HERE ARE FIVE PLACES IN *TANACH*, SAYS RASHI, WHERE YAAKOV *AVINU'S* name is written *malei,* complete with the letter *vav.* There are also five places in *Tanach* where the name of Eliyahu the Prophet is written *chaser,* (incomplete), as *Eliyah,* instead of *Eliyahu.* Explains Rashi: Yaakov took the *vav* out of Eliyahu's name as a guarantee that Eliyahu would come and herald the *Moshiach,* as a guarantee that indeed there would be a Redemption for his children!

The first of these five references of "*Yaakov*" with a *vav* is in the verse in *Parshas Bechukosai:* וזכרתי את בריתי יעקוב — "*And I shall remember the Covenant of Jacob, and also My Covenant with Isaac and also My Covenant with Abraham shall I remember, and I will remember the land [to bring the Redemption]* (Vayikra 26:42).

To understand what Rashi means it is important to note that all four remaining verses quoted by Rashi refer to the future Redemption of Israel in one way or another:

1. "*Thus said Hashem: 'Behold I will bring the captivity of Jacob's tents, and have mercy on his dwelling-places. . .'* " (Yirmiyahu 30:18).

2. "*Thus said Hashem: 'If My covenant be not with day and night, and if I have not appointed the ordinances of heaven and earth; then will I cast away the seed of Jacob, and David, My servant, so that I will not take any of his seed to be rulers over the seed of Abraham, Isaac, and Jacob; for I will cause*

_____

Rabbi Shulman, rav of Shaarei Shomayim Congregation, Toronto Canada, is a certified Mohel.

106 Ꙩ ENTERING THE COVENANT

their captivity to return, and have mercy upon them' " (*Yirmihayu* 33:25-26).

3. *"But as for you, fear not My servant Jacob, and be not dismayed, O Israel, for behold, I will save you from afar and your seed from the land of their captivity; and Jacob shall return, and be tranquil and at ease and none shall make him afraid."* (*Yirmiyahu* 46:27).

4. *"The portion of Jacob is not like them; for He is the former of all things and Israel, the tribe of His inheritance: His Name is Hashem, Master of Legions, is His name* (*Yirmiyahu* 51:19).

My grandfather, Rabbi Yechiel Michel Kossowsky *zt'l*, of Johannesburg, explained that since Yaakov led the Jews into exile, by bringing his family down to Egypt, it is he who demanded from Eliyahu, the harbinger of the *Moshiach,* that he guarantee to bring them out of exile in the future. On one level, therefore, linking Yaakov to Eliyahu links the beginning of our exile with its end.

But, this only begs a more fundamental question. Why is it necessary to have Eliyahu herald the *Moshiach* at all? And why specifically Eliyahu?

To this Rabbi Kossowsky suggested that the key characteristic that would bring the Jews out of exile would be that of *Mesiras Nefesh,* self-sacrifice for the sake of Torah. Eliyahu sacrificed his whole life for the sake of defending Torah. He fought a difficult battle to win back the hearts of the people to their Father in Heaven. It is only that kind of sincere commitment to Torah, educating the people to declare, ה' הוא האלקים — "Hashem is our G-d," as Eliyahu did on Mt. Carmel, that will bring our people back to G-d, and thus bring the *Moshiach.*

There is another connection between Eliyahu and the Redemption, however. Eliyahu is called the *Malach Ha'Bris,* the "Angel of the Covenant." Our Sages tell us that his spirit comes to every circumcision of every newborn Jewish boy. Eliyahu comes to each *Bris* in order to testify before the Almighty that the Jews have always shown total commitment and dedication to this *mitzvah,* at times with great *mesiras nefesh.* Eliyahu comes to testify that through our *mesiras nefesh* for this *mitzvah* we are indeed worthy of Redemption.

The Talmud says (*Menachos* 53b) that the Jews were not exiled from the land until they abandoned the *mitzvah* of circumcision. At the same time, the *Zohar* says (*Parshas Lech Lecha*) that the Jews shall return to the land of Israel through the merit of the *mitzvah* of circumcision. That is why Eliyahu is the harbinger of the *Moshiach.* He bears witness before G-d that the Jewish People have always been committed to this fundamental *mitz-*

vah, and it is his testimony as the *Malach Ha'Bris* that will ultimately allow us to merit the *Geulah Shleimah.*

Yaakov Avinu demanded a guarantee from Eliyahu, by demanding that Eliyahu continue to be present at every *Bris.* That way he could guarantee the future Redemption of Israel, through the *zechus* of the *mitzvah* of *Bris Milah.*

May we merit to see the coming of *Moshiach,* speedily in our days.

Sefer Bamidbar

פרשת במדבר
Parshas Bamidbar

_____ Harvey Wolinetz

THE POEM "YOM LEYABASHA" WRITTEN BY RABBI YEHUDAH HALEVI IS traditionally recited during the *Seudas Mitzvah* following a circumcision. The poem is recited at the *Bris* meal because of the reference made to the *Bris Milah* in the fifth and seventh stanzas and according to the *Yalkut Shimoni,* "Because the Jews had themselves circumcised they merited that Hashem split the Sea for them."

The fourth stanza of the Poem begins, "May You raise my banners over the survivors and may You gather the scattered ones . . ."

Rav Asher Anshil Grunwald in his *Zocher Habris* explains that we pray to Hashem that just as our banners were raised in the desert following the redemption from Egypt, so shall our banners be raised in our final redemption. He also refers to the sentence in *Yeshayahu* (62:10), הרימו נס על העמים — "Lift a banner over the Peoples." The *Me'am Lo'ez* explains that the Prophet is urging *Bnai Yisrael* to prepare for the final redemption by raising themselves to such spiritual heights so as to make themselves a "banner" to the nations.

What greater "banner" can a Jewish male carry that exemplifies *emunah* in God and demonstrates this fundamental belief to all the nations of the world, than the *Bris Milah*?

In *Parshas Bamidbar* (2:2) G-d instructs Moshe and Aharon that the Israelites shall encamp "every man by his banner having his paternal

---

Mr. Wolinetz is a real estate investor and former president of the Community Synagogue of Monsey New York.

family insignia." The banners, which delineated the various encampments, had a profound spiritual significance in addition to fulfilling the need of demarcating the locations of the various tribes. The Midrash tells us that it was *Bnai Yisrael* who requested the *degalim* (banners) after having prophetically envisioned them at Mt. Sinai during the giving of the Ten Commandments. They perceived G-d's descent upon the mountain accompanied by 22,000 chariots of angels who were divided in four groups, each flying a different banner. The Israelites wanted to recreate this feeling of holiness by using the banners to help them attain a higher level of attachment to Hashem. And G-d granted their request and had them set up their camps under four main banners.

There are many discussions and opinions as to what was displayed on each banner and whether or not there were sub-banners corresponding to the sub groupings delineated in the Chapter. But the true significance of the banners was the spiritual connection to G-d that it engendered, as envisioned by the Jews at Sinai. It was the spiritual uplifting that the Israelites in the desert yearned for and expected to achieve through the banners they perceived ushering the angels at Mt. Sinai and which they now fashioned for themselves.

The *Bris Milah* has been the banner that has always marked the location of the Jew in the world. The banners and their distinctive insignia which flew over the Jewish encampment had a spiritual significance that could not be replicated with just any banner. So too, a surgical circumcision cannot replace a *Bris Milah* which is imbued with a sacred importance that elevates the act of circumcision to one which brings the Jew closer to G-d.

King Solomon, in the *Song of Songs* (7:1) says that the nations of the world will say to the Jewish people "Return return, O Shulamite. . . ." the meaning of which is that we want *Klal Yisrael* to turn away and take on our beliefs and we will become united. The *Me'am Lo'ez* goes on to explain that the nations of the world even offer to make new banners for the Jewish people, but the offer is rejected because they know that the deeper spiritual significance of their original banners can not be reproduced by the nations of the world. Similarly, the spiritual essence of the *Bris Milah* cannot be reproduced by a circumcision performed by a surgeon.

Turnus Rufus, the Roman governor who put down the Bar Kochba rebellion 60 years after the destruction of the Second Temple, attempted to break the Jewish spirit by preventing the performance of *Bris Milah*.

Throughout our history other despots have also tried to nullify *Bris Milah*. By and large they have failed.

Today, we demonstrate our continuous and unending faith in Hashem and our continued efforts to achieve a greater closeness to Him by holding high the Banner of *Bris Milah*. Let us hope that *all* of our people will rally around this banner and Hashem will heed the words of the poet and "gather the scattered ones." May this allow *Moshiach* to readily find us and arrive speedily in our time.

פרשת נשא
Parshas Naso

_____ *Mandell I. Ganchrow, MD*

HOW APPROPRIATE IT IS ON THIS VERY SPECIAL DAY IN THE LIFE OF OUR newborn, our רך הנמול, that this week's *parshah* contains the Priestly Blessing יברכך ה׳ — "May Hashem bless you" (*Bamidbar* 6:24).

The Priestly Blessing segment of the *parshah* begins וידבר ה׳ אל משה לאמר — "Hashem spoke to Moses thus saying" and then Hashem in-structs Moshe, "Speak unto Aaron and his children saying," לאמר, repeat-ing the instruction once again. Says the *Orach Chaim*, this repetition of the word לאמר indicates an instruction not only for Moshe to the *Kohanim* of his generation, but they in turn have an obligation "לאמר" to convey the blessings to future generations of *Kohanim*.

The *Kesav Sofer* points out a beautiful thought that surely applies in this wonderful moment. When the *Kohanim* bless the Jewish people to be prosperous and successful there might possibly be an undertone of self-interest, for the *Kohanim* themselves were the beneficiaries of *Matnos Kehunah*, the special gifts that were given to the *Kohanim*. Therefore, Rashi says, אמור להם, "say to them" with *kavanah* — talk to them with complete sincerity and a full heart to impress upon them that the *be-rachah* that they are about to bestow upon the Jewish people will be for their benefit only and *not* for any self-enrichment. Consequently, says the *Kesav Sofer*, the instruction of G-d is given solely and directly to Aharon. We know that in the *midbar*, the custom of *Matnos Kehunah* had not yet been instituted. Therefore, the blessing entrusted to Aharon and through him to the *Kohanim* of future generations, was pure and selfless and solely for the benefit of the Jewish people. The preface כה תברכו, "so shall you bless" is instructional. In this manner, free of any thought of potential personal gain, shall future generations of *Kohanim* bless the Jewish people with the blessings that Aharon and the *Kohanim* uttered.

Today we celebrate a *Bris* of the newest member of *Am Yisrael*. The blessing that we all utter, that he should grow to Torah, *Chuppah*, and *Massim Tovim* is pronounced with purity, love in our hearts and without the slightest taint of jealousy or self-interest for our newest brother who joins us.

In the chapter immediately following this portion the Torah tells us, ויהי ביום כלות משה להקים את המשכן, that "it was on the day that Moshe concluded erecting the Tabernacle," they anointed and sanctified it, and its utensils. Rabbi Shmuel Tuvia Stern in his *sefer Ateret Zahav* notes that the word כלות represents perfection and can only be attributed to the works of G-d Himself. Thus, at the end of the six days of creation the Torah states, ויכלו השמים והארץ, "the heavens and earth were completed." The *Mishkan*, likewise, was constructed "על פי ה'", under the supervision of G-d and therefore warranted a seal of perfection. But human beings are imperfect by definition. Today, on the occasion of the *Bris Milah* the blessing that we bestow upon this child is that his entire life should be dedicated to striving for the highest level of perfection in his personal conduct to bring great glory to himself and his family.

פרשת בהעלתך
Parshas Beha'alosecha

Rabbi Joseph I. Singer

THE BIRTH OF A BELOVED SON AUGMENTS OUR FAMILY AND INCREASES OUR JOY. We thank Hashem for this gift of life and pray that our aspirations for him be amply realized.

In this week's _Sidrah_ we read about the complaints of those who were טמאי נפש, unclean, and therefore could not bring the Pesach offering. They complained to Moshe, למה נגרע, "Why should we be diminished" and not be able to celebrate our freedom by eating the Paschal lamb (_Bamidbar_ 9:7).

In the _Mesores Ha'Tanach_ of Rabbi Chaim Heller, _zt"l_ (which I edited) there is a marginal note referring to _Bamidbar_ 27:4, where the daughters of Zelophchad complain that since their father died without sons why should they, the daughters, be deprived of their father's estate — למה יגרע, why should the name of our father be omitted from among his family?

The favorable response to these two complaints created a new holiday and enfranchised daughters to receive an inheritance in the absence of sons. For those who were not permitted to observe the regular Passover holiday because they were unclean, a new holiday, _Pesach Sheini_ was instituted whereby they could offer the _Korban Pesach_ and eat it with _Matzoh_ and _Maror_. _Pesach Sheini_, which still is on our calendar, was established due to the justified complaints of people who did not want to be left out.

Rabbi Singer is rav of Manhattan Beach Jewish Center, Brooklyn, New York.

Likewise, the warranted complaint of the daughters of Zelophchad amended the inheritance law to have daughters share in the patrimony of their father.

We see from these two incidents how potent is the justified complaint of "למה נגרע„.

The parents are joyful because of the latest addition to their family. As they enter him into the covenant of Avraham they also affirm a personal covenant to train their child in the ways of Judaism — to observe its *mitzvos*, walk in the ways of G-d and develop all his talents to be a loving son. "למה נגרע," why should we be less?

From the time of their son's birth, the parents should feel as if G-d is telling them that He has given them a beautiful gift to be cherished and developed to the highest potential. They must enter him in the covenant of Avraham with the hope and prayer of doing the ultimate to attain maximum fulfillment.

Not only do we wish them spiritual success, but also material bounties.

Instead of "למה נגרע„ — may the parents and family receive unlimited joy and infinite *nachas* from this latest addition to the family.

פרשת שלח
Parshas Shelach

_____ Rabbi Dr. Morton J. Summer

In *Parshas Shelach* we are told of the report that the *meraglim* (spies) gave to the Children of Israel when they returned to the desert from their expedition to Eretz Yisrael. They had been sent by Moshe *Rabbeinu* to reconnoiter the land of Canaan, its inhabitants, and armies. Ten of the spies returned with a devastating message that broke the morale of *Klal Yisrael*. They said, "The people that dwell in the land are fierce and the cities are fortified and very great" (*Bamidbar* 13:28). They embellished this by saying, "We are not able to go up against the people for they are stronger than we" (v.31).

Several questions are raised: What impelled the spies to argue so vehemently against the proposed ascent to the land of Canaan? Moreover, why was their message so calamitous to *Klal Yisrael*? Had not the people witnessed the great miracles leading to the *geulah* — the Ten Plagues and the splitting of the Red Sea? Did they not see the miracles of heavenly provisions on demand — the manna and the well — as well as the water that emerged from the stones? These occurrences did not require blind belief and faith for they had *seen* them happen before their very eyes. How could the report of these ten mortals outweigh the testimony and experiences of hundreds of thousands of men, women, and children? Surely what G-d had done to the Egyptians and Amalekites He could visit upon the Canaanites in due time. Even more pointedly, the Lubavitcher

_____
Rabbi Dr. Summer is a retired educator living in Monsey, New York.

Rebbe *zt"l* asks, why when Calev tries to counter their calumnies did he not mention to *Klal Yisrael* these recent miracles? They surely would have been the most convincing proof of this case. Yet Calev says only, "We shall go up and inherit the land for we are able to overcome it" (v. 30). Was Calev perhaps in doubt of G-d's ability to vanquish the Canaanites? It goes without saying that this is too ridiculous an assumption to even consider.

The Rebbe suggests the following explanation: The *meraglim* were not driven by dread of defeat in battle. What they feared was a spiritual downfall. In the *midbar*, all the Israelite's needs were supplied directly by Hashem. They did not have to expend any effort in acquiring their food or water. Their bread, the manna, fell at their doorway, water came to their tent from Miriam's well, and their clothes never needed mending. Conquering the land of Israel meant that food, water, clothes, and defense would be their own responsibility. Each of these needs would require effort, labor, and concern.

The *meraglim* were special people chosen by Moshe *Rabbeinu* for the purpose of allaying the fears of many Israelites about the conquest and inheritance of the promised land. The *meraglim*'s worry was that the burden of working the land and making a living would eventually leave *Klal Yisrael* with diminished time and energy for the service of Hashem and the study of His Torah. They said, "It is a land which eats up its inhabitants," meaning that the land and its attendant requirements would consume all the energies of the Israelites. The *meraglim* held that יראת שמים and Torah flourish when there is freedom from the challenging needs of daily life. They wanted a secluded wilderness existence where even the food was from heaven.

Contemporary life has many instances of individuals and groups who indeed conceive of a form of Torah life that can only exist and flourish in a separatist environment, secluded from confrontations with modern life. However, the spies were as wrong then as are those who follow in their footsteps today. The Rebbe asserts that the goal of a life governed by Torah and *Mitzvos* is not merely the elevation of the soul and preparation for *Olam Haba*, it is mainly for the sanctification of this world, the *olam hazeh*. The purpose of each *mitzvah* individually and of the *Taryag mitzvos* collectively, is to bring Hashem into this world and not to leave Him hovering above us in Heaven. A *mitzvah* is designed to locate the immanence of G-d in the natural world, not in the supernatural. The miracles in the desert were not the epitome of other worldly spirituality, they were designed to raise *Klal Yisrael* to a spiritual level that would facilitate the conquest of the land Canaan and transform it into the holy land of Israel. Herein was the error of the *meraglim*. They saw the desert wilderness as the natural habitat of holiness untrammeled by the challenges of a dynamically developing society. In fact, however, the miracles inherent in sanctifying the real life of the here and now are even more miraculous than the supernatural events that had occurred in the *midbar*.

Joshua and Calev did not calm the Israelites' fears by reminding them of the miracles they had seen in the desert, for those miracles came in a different sphere and on a unique level. However, in crossing the Jordan River they would pass into a life that would endow time and place, the finite world of toil and tears, with the sanctity of Hashem. Calev's answer to the ten spies was, "Let us go up, let us indeed go up and inherit the land." As the Rebbe explains," let us go up" is said twice. We have already ascended to the spirituality of the wilderness, we have risen above the concerns of the world. Let us now make a new and greater ascent, finding the holiness of G-d within the world itself.

The lesson of Calev's argument is that spirituality is not a concealed possession that should not be shared with the world. Instead, its essence manifests itself when a Jew reaches out beyond himself to his fellow Jew. In the world of man's work, he extends holiness to everything he touches, without fear that he is endangering his faith, without thinking that any context or situation lies outside G-d's dominion. Unfortunately, *Klal Yisrael* did not accept Calev's argument and were punished with an additional forty years of wandering in the desert but with diminished holiness and recurring quarreling and rebellions against Hashem.

The *mitzvah* of *Bris Milah*, while incumbent on the father, is the first act involving the baby himself in service to Hashem. There are three partners in the creation of a child: Hashem, the father, and the mother (*Kiddushin* 30b). The child's first response to the call of Hashem will be the response to his father's voice. The Midrash in *Shemos* relates that Hashem called to Moshe in the voice of his father Amram so that Moshe would not be frightened. When Moshe heard, "Moshe, Moshe," he answered, "Yes, Father." Hashem said, "I am not your father, I am the G-d of your father." The father represents the voice of Hashem to the child and ideally the youngster should not be able to distinguish between the voice of Hashem and that of his parents. The *Bris Milah* imprints the seal of the covenant on the child. It is the father's first declaration and charge to his child to join the covenental community of Avraham's descendants.

May the רך הנמול continue to develop in *olam hazeh* — performing *mitzvos*, demonstrating יראת שמים and love of Torah in this world. His purpose should always be to bring the *kedushah* of Hashem into *olam hazeh,* into the right here and now. This, ultimately, will bring him to sanctify *Olam Haba*, the World to Come.

פרשת קרח
Parshas Korach

— for a *Pidyon Haben*

Rabbi Sidney Shoham

*P*ARSHAS *KORACH* IS FILLED WITH REBELLION AND INTRIGUE. KORACH AND HIS followers feel that the prerogatives of their birthright were usurped by the *Kohanim* and *Levi'im*. Moshe is again faced with a new challenge and, as ever before, Hashem comes to his rescue. Near the conclusion of the *parshah*, we have the *mitzvah* of *Pidyon Haben*: פדה תפדה את בכור האדם — "But you shall surely redeem the firstborn of man" (*Bamidbar* 18:15).

What is the purpose of *Pidyon Haben*? Why does the concept extend into the animal kingdom and why are the gifts to the *Kohanim* (18:8-19) — portions from *Korbanos, terumah* from the crops, firstborn male sons and firstborn male Kosher animals — found in *Parshas Korach*?

Let us attempt to understand the purpose of *mitzvos* in general. Primarily, it is to make us cognizant of the presence of Hashem as sole creator and master of the universe and all of its inhabitants. Hashem continues to be the creator of destiny in all facets of endeavor as we recite in the *Shacharis* prayer, "In Your goodness, You renew creation constantly on a daily basis."

One of the most startling moments in the life of a human being is witnessing the first fruit of a newly planted tree or field. Likewise, if one possesses an animal and sees it bear its first offspring, this results in a feeling of intense joy and satisfaction. How much more so when parents experience the birth of their firstborn son. They feel the awe and wonderment of nature to the highest degree. They have become partners in G-d's creation mode and have reached the status of the צלם אלקים, image of

---

Rabbi Shoham is rav of Beth Zion Congregation, Cote St. Luc, Quebec, Canada.

122   ENTERING THE COVENANT

G-d — with the will of Hashem they have become creators with Him. "*Tzelem Elokim*" becomes a reality in their lives.

In contrast, we find that the last of the Ten Plagues was the smiting of the first-born. The Egyptians worshipped their first offspring as a form of idolatry. G-d did not enter the picture. *Klal Yisrael* leaves Egypt with an everlasting message of faith and commitment. Everything in life is a gift from Hashem and the birth of the nation of Israel begins with the smiting of idolatry. The Exodus exemplifies a new way of life that would shortly be expounded at Mt. Sinai.

Pidyon Haben is one example of a *mitzvah* that recognizes the source of all human existence. We humble ourselves and admit with joy that all of our actions are only with the help and will of Hashem. The interaction of the father and *Kohen* in the act of redemption personifies this message. The beginning of all life is a gift. What we treasure most comes from a source outside of ourselves. The first fruits of the land are to be shared with the *Kohanim* and *Levi'im* and presented as gifts to reward them for their service and allegiance. The portion describing the gifts to the *Kohanim* and *Levi'im* is specifically mentioned here after Korach's rebellion and challenge. It proves unequivocally that Hashem recognizes and appreciates them as His most loyal servants.

On the other hand, Korach wishes to usurp his birthright. He reacted beyond the will of G-d and challenged Moshe for position and power. Primarily, he was concerned with his self-image and hunger for leadership. The result was that he was swallowed up by the very earth that through Hashem was the source of man's creation (עפר מן האדמה). Little wonder that in *Pirkei Avos* (5:20) we read, "Which controversy was not in the name of Heaven? The controversy of Korach and his company."

When a *bechor* is born, we redeem him through a *Kohen* and with all our heart and soul say to Hashem, "Thank You." We stand in awe and wonderment and pray to Hashem that the child who is now ours to hold and to keep should have a wonderful and long life עד מאה ועשרים שנה, "for one hundred and twenty years."

Mazel Tov.

פרשת חקת
Parshas Chukas

_____ *Rabbi Zvi Karpel*

T HIS WEEK'S *PARSHAH* OF *CHUKAS* CONVEYS TWO VITAL MESSAGES FOR OUR newborn and his family. The first involves the *mitzvah* of the פרה אדומה (red cow) as described in the beginning of our *parshah*; the second revolves around the incident of Moshe *Rabbeinu* striking the rock to procure water for the *Bnai Yisrael* in the wilderness.

Let us first consider the *mitzvah* of the פרה אדומה. To put this *mitzvah* into the proper framework, we should consider that generally, the *mitzvos* of the Torah can be grouped into one of three broad categories: עדות, משפטים, חוקים. The first, עדות, are *mitzvos* that testify either to an historical event or to some aspect of *emunah*, or belief. עדות is translated as testimonies and can be understood in a logical manner. One prime example, is the *mitzvah* of observing the Shabbos. This attests to our belief that G-d created the world in six days. The second category of *mitzvos*, משפטים or civil laws, are Divine laws that relate to the safety and survival of society. Prime examples of משפטים are theft and murder. Perhaps, even more so than עדות, משפטים can easily be comprehended for their obvious impact on maintaining a society that respects moral rectitude and values.

The third category of חוקים, or Divine ordinances is the concern of our *parshah*, from which it derives its name. The purpose or meaning behind each חוק cannot readily be understood by a rationally thinking person. The logic of this *mitzvah* is purely Divine. According to Rashi's explanation of

_____
Rabbi Karpel is the chaplain at Daughters of Israel Geriatric Center, West Orange, New Jersey.

the word "חוק,, in the beginning of the parshah, a חוק is a decree, a law which the Torah requires us to accept without question because we, as humans, are not capable of comprehending it. The law of the פרה אדומה involved using the ashes of a red heifer to cleanse a particular person from being ritually impure (טמא), and making him pure (טהור), once again. Moreover, another aspect of the ritual entailed anyone involved in preparing the ashes as becoming טמא. This complicates the issue and makes it even more incomprehensible. According to the Midrash, when Hashem taught Moshe *Rabbeinu* that a Jew becomes טמא through physical contact with a dead body, Moshe questioned Him as to how that person can once again become pure. At first, the Almighty declined to provide Moshe with an answer. However, later that day, Hashem explained to both Moshe and Aharon that someone who had become defiled by contact with a corpse could become pure again by sprinkling him with a special mixture of water and ashes from a red heifer. This delay was actually a *chesed* to Aharon who had not been present when Moshe first asked the question. The fact that Hashem waited and replied when both were present indicated that He had in fact forgiven Aharon for his part in the sin of the Golden Calf.

The lessons that can be drawn from the *parshah* of the פרה אדומה are fundamental to Judaism. Firstly, not every *mitzvah* can be understood by the limited scope of human intelligence. One of the tenets of our faith is that Hashem is infinite, both in His existence and in His wisdom. Conversely, man is finite both in his existence and in his wisdom. As Rav Yochanan explained to his students in regard to their failure to understand the laws of the פרה אדומה: "It is not the corpse that causes contamination or the ashes of the cow that causes purity. These laws are decrees of G-d, and man has no right to question them."

The second aspect of the *parshah* that I wish to discuss in relation to affording a lesson for our newborn is the incident of Moshe striking the rock in Midbar Zin following the death of Miriam. In the beginning of Chapter 20, the people protest to Moshe and Aharon once again about the lack of water. Hashem tells Moshe: "Take the staff and gather together the assembly, you and Aharon your brother, and speak to the rock before their eyes that it shall give its waters" (20:8). After gathering the people together, Moshe says "Listen now, O rebels, shall we bring forth water for you from this rock?" (v. 10). In the next verse we are told that Moshe raises his arm and strikes the rock twice. Water comes forth in abundance and the people and animals drink from it.

The commentators offer diverse opinions as to what exactly was the nature of the sin. According to Rashi, the sin was in striking the rock rather than speaking to it. On the other hand, the Rambam maintains that Moshe's sin was in becoming angry. This was exacerbated by the people's assumption that Moshe's anger reflected Hashem's anger. But nowhere do we find any evidence of Hashem's anger. A third view, held by the Ramban and R'Chananel, is that Moshe missed the opportunity to sanctify Hashem's Name. The key words that they point to in the text are, "Shall we bring forth water . . . ?" This phrase implied that Moshe and Aharon had the power to produce water. Clearly, Moshe should have said, "Shall Hashem bring forth?" Moshe *Rabbeinu* disobeyed Hashem's command. He also displayed a bad trait by becoming angry at the people. This was a drawback in his leadership. Finally, he missed a golden opportunity to perform a *Kiddush Hashem* in the way he conducted himself. Moshe's sin caused him to be denied entry into the Promised Land. Rashi states in *Parshas Matos* that it was Moshe's anger that caused him to err in judgment and to strike the rock.

This crucial incident in the Torah holds a tremendous lesson for our newborn. As he goes through life, he will confront many challenges. Everything will not always go smoothly for him. Yet, he must always keep his cool and be levelheaded. Anger is a terrible *midah* that can lead to ill-advised actions. We learn from what happened to Moshe, that the ends do not always justify the means. There is a proper way to do things, especially when it concerns a leadership role. The blessing that I give the newborn as he enters this special covenant between G-d and the Jewish people, is that he should be *zocheh* to find ways to perform a *Kiddush Hashem* when the opportunity arises. He should merit to be able to act properly, and keep his negative emotions in check. May he be *zocheh* to always appreciate all of the *mitzvos*, no matter what category they may be in.

May his parents be *zocheh* to raise this child to Torah, *Chuppah* and *Maasim Tovim*. Mazel tov.

פרשת בלק
Parshas Balak

Rabbi Mordechai Willig

"AND NOW . . . I WILL ADVISE YOU" (24:14). RASHI, CITING SANHEDRIN (106a), tells us what Bilam's advice to Balak was. Since Hashem hates promiscuity, Bilam suggested that they should induce the Israelite men to sin. This strategy, attributed to Bilam (31:16) proved successful and caused 24,000 to die in a plague (25:1,9). The zealous act of Pinchas halted the plague by turning back Hashem's anger, and earned him the covenant of peace (25:7-12).

Every _bris_ ceremony begins with the words which describe the heroism of Pinchas, and the subsequent reward of _"Brisi Shalom."_ Why were these _pesukim_ chosen? Furthermore, why was Bilam's strategy successful at this particular time, a point alluded to in his opening word — and now (ועתה)?

Rav C. Y. Goldwicht, _zt"l,_ answered the latter question based on Rashi (23:8) who quotes _Sanhedrin_ (105b). Bilam's power was that he knew the precise moment that Hashem is angry every day. But all the days that Bilam came to Balak, Hashem did not get angry at all.

Generally, anger is a negative attribute. Why, then, does Hashem exhibit anger every day? Apparently, anger, which is a manifestation of strict justice (_din_) and strength (_gevurah_), is necessary, albeit in very small measure, to create a balance in the Heavens with Hashem's dominant attribute of kindness (_chessed_).

An unchecked overabundance of _chessed_ can lead to temptations of

Rabbi Willig is rav of the Young Israel of Riverdale and a rosh yeshiva at Yeshivas Rabbeinu Yitzchak Elchanan in New York City.

immorality (עריות — see *Vayikra* 20:17). Bilam was frustrated at the complete absence of Hashem's anger for many days, which prevented him from cursing *Am Yisrael*. He sensed that the lack of anger created an imbalance, an overabundance of *chessed*, which would make people more susceptible to the temptations of immortality. Thus his cunning, and successful advice that **now** was the right time to entice the men of *Am Yisrael* to commit a sin which is a perversion of *chessed*.

To this interpretation of the Rosh Yeshiva zt"l, one may add the following: Why was Hashem's anger so powerful as to threaten the very existence of our people and how did the act of Pinchas quell this anger? Perhaps, there was, כביכול (as it were), a measure of pent-up anger because of all the days when no anger was shown. This posed a grave threat when the men of *Am Yisrael* succumbed to the sin of *zenus*.

Pinchas is introduced as the grandson of Aharon, a man who personifies love and the pursuit of peace (אוהב שלום ורודף שלום). When Pinchas, of all people, overcame his inherited predisposition to avoid controversy, and zealously avenged the crime on behalf of Hashem, the balance was restored and Hashem's anger abated.

The reward that Pinchas received, *Brisi Shalom*, seems inappropriate for an act of violence. In reality, however, a peace without principles cannot stand. Pinchas, by fighting for principle, and by utilizing an attribute that was antithetical to his personality and upbringing, achieved true *shalom*.

At every *Bris*, a father overcomes his innate, overwhelming and unconditional love for his son, and performs, by proxy, what has been called a barbaric act. Thus, the appropriate introduction to the *Bris* is the similar, though much more heroic and dramatic, action of Pinchas. Perhaps the parallel of *Brisi Shalom*, the reward of Pinchas, is the proper balance of discipline and unconditional love required for successful parenting.

The Rambam (*Moreh Nevuchim* 3:49) suggests that a reason for *Bris Milah* is the curbing of the male desire, which enables a Jewish man to resist the temptation of immorality. If so, the introduction of Pinchas' zealousness is directly on point. As noted earlier, the males of *Am Yisrael* sinned because the balance of *chessed* and *gevurah* was impaired by the absence of Hashem's anger. Pinchas' zealousness restored that balance and saved us from Hashem's wrath.

Similarly, a *Bris*, according to the Rambam, is necessary to achieve a proper balance to ensure that the powerful male *yetzer hara* be held in check. Therefore, the preceding *pesukim* describing how Pinchas achieved this critical balance are quoted as the appropriate introduction to each *Bris Milah*.

Sadly, in our times, society has lost its sense of balance and proportion in these areas. Parenting in America generally avoids placing limitations on the activities of children. In Israel, spanking a misbehaving youngster, a Biblically (*Mishlei* 13:24) mandated and Talmudically (*Makkos* 8a) sanctioned act, has been criminalized by the court. While overly restricting a child is inadvisable, and hitting too hard or often is prohibited, the nearly total absence of discipline has led to a situation in which the traditional balance of proper child rearing has been lost.

The decadence and permissiveness of modern society poses a threat to all of our children. At a *Bris*, when we invoke the *pesukim* describing Pinchas's act and its reward, we should be mindful of the lessons that apply to all generations. By learning these lessons and acting upon them, parents can raise their children in the traditional, balanced way and thereby be blessed, as was Pinchas, with the *berachah* of peace, *shalom*.

פרשת פינחס
Parshas Pinchas

——————————————————————— *Rabbi Moshe D. Krupka*

This week's *Sidrah* is fundamentally linked to *Bris Milah*. As a newborn baby is brought toward the *Kisei shel Eliyahu*, the *mohel* (in most traditions) quotes directly from the beginning of *Parshas Pinchas*: "Hashem spoke to Moses, saying: 'Pinchas, son of Elazar, the son of Aaron the *Kohen*, withdrew My anger from the Children of Israel, by zealously avenging Me, so that I did not destroy the Children of Israel in My vengeance. Therefore, say: Behold, I give him My covenant of peace.' "(*Bamidbar* 25:10-12).

These *pesukim* follow an episode where, as a result of Balak's attempts (based on Bilam's advice) to lead the *Bnai Yisrael* towards idolatry, Zimri, a prince of the tribe of Simeon, consorted with a Midianite woman in public. Moshe and the elders were reduced to weeping, because they realized that the people were caught up in a frenzy of rebellion, which ultimately provoked Hashem's wrath via a devastating plague. Some *Meforshim* explain that the leadership may have felt that any protest on their part would merely fuel the people's rebelliousness.

Pinchas, however, was driven to action. He killed Zimri and the woman. As a result, the plague which Hashem had inflicted upon the *Bnai Yisrael* because of their involvement with the Moabite and Midianite women was halted. Pinchas was rewarded for his actions by being forever linked to the *Bris Shalom*, the "covenant of peace." Literally, Rashi says this means that he was appointed as a *Kohen* (up to that point, only Aharon and his sons

———————————————

Rabbi Krupka is National Director of Synagogue Community Services, Orthodox Union.

had been made *Kohanim*, and any further children born to them would be *Kohanim* from birth). He also merited mention in the ceremony of *Bris Milah*. In fact, the *Midrash* points out that *Bris Shalom* refers to the ultimate *Bris* between Hashem and His people, the *Bris* of Avraham *Avinu*, i.e. the *Bris Milah*.

This raises several questions. Firstly, why was Pinchas, who committed the most violent act possible, rewarded with something so diametrically opposed to his action, the *Bris Shalom*?

Secondly, Pinchas, was not the only person who managed to subdue Hashem's anger; in fact Moshe did so several times (for example, after the episode of the Golden Calf and the episode of the Spies), but he was not rewarded with the same recognition. In this case, there must be something unique that we learn from Pinchas' actions. What special traits should we be aware of which gave him the merit of being invoked and forever associated with each and every *Bris Milah*?

Menachem Mendel of Kotzk explained that children are taught that Pinchas was a "zealot." Perhaps the simple view is that he was some kind of extremist. If so, how do we see his actions in a positive light? In fact, says the Kotzker, Pinchas acted decisively at a time when others shook their heads in confusion or tutted in silent condemnation. What must also be made clear is that his actions were premeditated. He did not rise up in the heat of the moment and in his anger, "take matters into his own hands."

Rashi says that Pinchas saw what Zimri had done, and consulted with his Rebbe, Moshe, asking him what the appropriate response was according to *halachah*. Providence made Moshe forget the answer, but Pinchas knew from his own depth of learning that the Torah punishment for this abominable indiscretion states, "a zealous one may slay him." The text says that "he got up from amongst the people" — Pinchas was not motivated simply by abstract Torah scholarship, but acted out of deep concern and love for his fellow man. In saying that he arose from amongst the people, the text implies that he was a man who was intrinsically involved with *Bnai Yisrael* on an individual level, and was deeply moved by seeing them become ensnared in immorality.

Avraham *Avinu* was the first Jew to enter into Hashem's *Bris Shalom*. The Rambam in *Hilchos Avodas Kochavim* states that the one factor that encapsulated Avraham's whole personality was his ability to **act**. Everywhere that he went, he affected people by his actions; he was a man who "wore his religion on his sleeve." By incorporating his relationship with

Hashem into everything that he did, he took his spirituality out of the abstract and into a reality that others could relate to and emulate. Similarly, Pinchas was elevated above his peers. His outstanding commitment to Hashem and dedication to His Torah, along with his love of *Klal Yisrael*, meant that he decisively found out what needed to be done, and then acted without delay.

In this way, we can understand zealotry as a *positive* attribute. A zealot by Torah standards is someone who is motivated for the right reasons, and takes the appropriate action, based on Torah values and love for *Klal Yisrael*. It is only then that one's actions can bring about *shalom*.

My *berachah* to the new baby is that he should grow to learn Torah and perform *mitzvos*. May he be involved on a personal level for the good of *Klal Yisrael*, and all his actions should be motivated by commitment, dedication and *kovod* for Hashem and His Torah. Mazel Tov.

פרשת מטות־מסעי
Parshas Matos-Masei

Rabbi Max N. Schreier

IN _PARSHAS MATOS_ (CHAPTER 32), WE READ OF THE APPROACH OF THE TWO tribes — the children of Gad and the children of Reuven — to Moshe requesting permission to settle on the other side of the Jordan (east bank) because the land was good for their livestock. Moshe responded to their request angrily and said to them, האחיכם יבאו למלחמה ואתם תשבו פה — "Should your brethren go out to war while you settle here?" (_Bamidbar_ 32:6). Even after they agreed to fight together with their brothers and help them conquer the land before settling themselves on the east bank, Moshe still imposed strict conditions upon them.

Why was Moshe so reluctant to agree to a request that made sense in terms of the economic interests of the tribes of Gad and Reuven?

I once heard from the Chief Rabbi of Jerusalem, the late Rabbi Bezalel Zolty, _zt"l,_ the following meaningful interpretation. He said that when it comes to Eretz Yisrael a person must not have conditions or _cheshbonos._ He must not have calculations to say that I will go to Israel if my income is guaranteed, or other some similar pragmatic thoughts.

What is true with regard to the _mitzvah_ of _Yishuv_ Eretz Yisrael, the settling of the land of Israel, is true of other _mitzvos_ as well.

Bris Milah, the entry into the covenant of Abraham, was a _mitzvah_ that Avraham entered as a sign of his commitment to G-d, without any other practical consideration.

This is the meaning that many give to the response that the assembled at a _Bris_ utter when the father of the child makes the _berachah_ להכניסו

Rabbi Schreier is rav of the Avenue N Jewish Center in Brooklyn, New York.

כשם שנכנס לברית כן יכנס בבריתו של אברהם אבינו. Everyone then responds, לתורה ולחפה ולמעשים טובים — Just as the child entered the *Bris Milah* in purity, in devotion to fulfill the G-dly command, so shall he enter the (study of) Torah, marriage and all the good deeds, without any calculation.

Rabbi Joseph. B. Soloveichik, *zt"l,* commented that the *Mohel* does not say that he is performing the *act* of circumcision, למול. Rather, he says על המילה — it is the *tachlis*, the *purpose* of the *mitzvah* that the child be מהול, that he be dedicated to G-dliness. This is not limited only to the time of the *Bris*, but is applicable to his entire life.

Indeed, this is the blessing that we impart to the רך הנמול and to his family. May they merit to see this child grow up to be a *ben Torah*, and a sincere practitioner of *mitzvos* in the same manner that he entered the *Bris*.

Sefer Devarim

פרשת דברים
Parshas Devarim

_____ *Rabbi Steven M. Dworken*

THE JOURNEY TO ERETZ YISRAEL, WHICH CONSTITUTES PART OF THIS WEEK'S *sedrah,* begins with an unusual statement of Moshe, who tells *Bnai Yisrael (Devarim* 1:6-7): ה׳ אלקינו דבר אלינו בחרב לאמר רב לכם שבת בהר הזה פנו וסעו לכם — "Hashem, our G-d, spoke to us in Chorev, saying, 'You have dwelt long enough at this mountain,' turn now [from Har Sinai] and begin traveling." Rashi comments, "the verse can be understood according to the plain meaning of the *pasuk* (כפשוטו)." Then *Rashi* brings a midrash: הרבה גדולה לכם ושכר על ישיבתכם בהר הזה. עשיתם משכן, מנורה, וכלים. קבלתם תורה, מניתם לכם סנהדרין שרי אלפים ושרי מאות.

The *peshat* would indicate that it's time for *Klal Yisrael* to move on to reach their final destination — our home — Eretz Yisrael. However, the midrash seems to be giving us a much deeper meaning. One should not think that *Bnai Yisrael* have dwelled long enough at Har Sinai or that they should leave Har Sinai behind as they move towards a new destination. Instead, they must remember רב לכם — "You have accomplished much here." The midrash quoted in Rashi states: "There is much eminence and reward for your having dwelt at this mountain — the *Mishka*n was built; the *keilim,* the utensils, including the *Menorah* were fashioned; the Torah was received; a Jewish judicial system was inaugurated." All of these accomplishments that symbolize the eternal message of *Yahadus,* must now be taken with *Bnai Yisrael* as they journey

_____

Rabbi Dworken is Executive Vice President of the Rabbinical Council of America, New York City.

to the promised land. Not only was *Bnai Yisrael* spared physical destruction in the desert, but they rose to great spiritual heights and achieved significant accomplishments. These values both in a physical and spiritual sense will not, and cannot, be abandoned during the journey forward. Instead, they are to be the foundation upon which future Jewish life will be built.

As the baby enters into the Covenant of Abraham, his parents and family must take upon themselves the prime and foremost responsibility to transmit the Torah way of life, our great traditions and accomplishments to yet another link in the chain of Judaism. The רב לכם in the sense of accomplishing a lot must be passed on. May this קטן become a גדול — an independent, strong and committed practitioner of Torah, *Avodah,* and *Gemilus Chasadim.*

פרשת ואתחנן
Parshas Va'eschanan

Rabbi A. Mark Levin

THE TORAH (*DEVARIM* 4:41) DESCRIBES HOW MOSHE *RABBEINU* DESIGNATED three Cities of Refuge (ערי מקלט) in Transjordan (**east** bank of the Jordan River) to which an unintentional killer could flee to find refuge from those seeking revenge. Moshe did so with the full knowledge that his act of designation was futile because the ערי מקלט only became operative and functional as Cities of Refuge when the other three cities on the **west** bank of the Jordan were likewise designated. This was beyond Moshe *Rabbeinu*'s grasp because he was not fated to ever cross over the **west** bank of the Jordan.

That being the case, asks Rashi (loc.cit), why did he do this futile act that had no practical application? Paraphrasing the Talmud (*Makkos* 10a), Rashi suggests Moshe *Rabbeinu*'s reasoning: "Any *mitzvah* that it is possible to fulfill, I will fulfill" — Such was the extent of Moshe's love for *mitzvos* that he wanted to perform as many as possible.

The *Kli Yakar* infers from Rashi's answer an insightful and very human principle: Many people are reluctant to undertake projects that they do not envisage completing. Hence, many worthwhile ideas and projects never see the light of day and remain stillborn because their completion and fulfillment may be beyond the scope of a lifetime or the abilities of the individual.

Rabbi Levin is Director, Rabbinic Placement, and Director, Gertrude & Morris Bienenfeld Department of Rabbinic Services at the Max Stern Division of Communal Services, at the Rabbi Isaac Elchanan Theological Seminary, an affiliate of Yeshiva University, New York City.

A similar thought is expressed in the Talmud (*Taanis* 23a) in the well-known story of the passerby who noticed an elderly person planting a sapling carob tree. "How long will it take before the tree bears fruit?" asked the passerby. "Possibly 70 years," answered the planter. "Are you so confident that you will live that long to benefit from the fruits and all your labor?" derided the passerby (expressing the point of view that "if I cannot benefit from my project, what is the point of even beginning it").

Answered the planter: "In the same way that I find in my world mature fruit-bearing trees from which I benefit without having invested in them, so do I want to bequeath to those who follow me, a world in which they will find mature fruit-bearing trees."

One possible interpretation is: Are we humans so self-centered and egotistical that we can only think of our own immediate self-gratification? Or, can we transcend our own need for immediate gratification, and unselfishly embrace future generations unknown to us, and assume a measure of responsibility for them as well?

An additional interpretation is: Are we capable of generating energy and enthusiasm only for those projects whose fruits we will enjoy? Or, are we capable of developing traits of patience and perseverance, simply by initiating and nurturing a project whose completion we will not witness (like Moshe *Rabbeinu* — "Any *mitzvah* that it is possible to fulfill, I will fulfill")?

It is a wonderful and special privilege to share in your *simcha* at the *Bris Milah / Pidyon Haben* of your son. Like every parent you express the very same commitment as that of Moshe *Rabbeinu*: "Any *mitzvah* that it is possible to fulfill, I will fulfill" (even though I am not able to fulfill or complete it in its entirety). With Hashem's help and blessing, you, too have commenced a *mitzvah* whose outcome and completion are beyond your ken: Will this child be blessed with health? Will he mature and be a *mensch*? Will he grow into a *ben Torah*? Will he mature into a thoughtful, caring, sensitive, loving human being?

While you may not be blessed with the privilege of *completing* the *mitzvah* (indeed, can any parent claim that they have truly completed the *mitzvah*?!), unlike Moshe *Rabbeinu,* you do have the wonderful opportunity and challenge of significantly advancing the *mitzvah*. As responsible parents you will be confronted with daily, no, hourly, choices calling for decisions that will impact on your son and his development.

That you, his parents, are yourselves loving, caring human beings in whose lives Torah, *Mitzvos,* acts of *Chessed* and *Tzedakah* are concrete, real and integral — in itself constitutes a wonderful model for your son to emulate.

That you, his parents are deeply involved in *Tzorchei Tzuibbur* — Synagogue, Yeshiva Day School, the broader community — will surely impact on him.

More difficult will be the challenge of determining (to the extent that parents can) the other factors and people that will impact on him: who will be his Rebbes and teachers; who will be his friends and peer reference group; as well as the other influences he will be exposed to, and more!

As parents, you embody the vision, determination, commitment, and idealism, of a Moshe *Rabbeinu* — to begin the *mitzvah* that requires the most patience and perseverance and an even greater investment of time, energy, love and resources (spiritual, emotional, material), of anything else. Not only that but the fruits might only blossom in the distant future. Such an essential undertaking and commitment require real spiritual strength.

May Hashem continue to grace you with health, energy, strength and wisdom to nurture your new infant son into a mature, healthy, spiritual personality.

May you witness and experience abundant *nachas* and the maximum fulfillment of this great *mitzvah* for many years to come.

פרשת עקב
Parshas Eikev

———————————————— *Rabbi Yitzchok Rosenberg*

"... AND HASHEM, — ושמר ה' אלקיך לך את הברית ואת החסד אשר נשבע לאבתיך your G-d shall keep the covenant with you and the kindness that He swore to your forefathers" (*Devarim* 7:12).

According to the Sforno, this refers to the *Bris* between Hashem and the Children of Israel when He commanded Avraham to perform the *Bris Milah*.

It seems that there was a physical act and a commitment to carry out *Mitzvos Maasios* — physical commandments. ומלתם את ערלת לבבכם — "And you shall circumcise the foreskin (barrier) of your heart ... " (*Devarim* 10:16).

"The foreskin of the heart" seems to connote, according to Rashi, a *spiritual* barrier which separates us from Hashem and requires a "circumcision" in order to allow us to reach our spiritual potential " ... The evil inclination has seven names, Moshe called it 'uncircumcised' (ערל) as it says, "You shall circumcise the foreskin of your heart" (*Sukkah* 52).

In what manner is the evil inclination like a foreskin? The Talmud (*Nedarim* 31b) teaches that if one vows not to receive any benefit from those who are uncircumcised, he may still derive benefit from an uncircumcised Jew and may not derive benefit from an uncircumcised idol worshipper. If he vows not to receive any benefit from those who are circumcised, he may not receive benefit from an uncircumcised Jew but

———————————
Rabbi Rosenberg is Director, Educational Programming, Division of Synagogue Services, Orthodox Union.

may benefit from a circumcised idol worshipper; for the term, "uncircumcised," is used only as a reference to the idol worshipper as it says, "For all of the nations are uncircumcised . . . " (*Jeremiah* 9:25). We see then that the term, "uncircumcised," is a description of a particular category of individual, even in the case where it seems to contradict fact and reality — i.e. even a circumcised idol worshipper is called "uncircumcised."

So too, it is true with the evil inclination — but there appears to be a paradox. Our Sages have taught, "Behold it was very good," this refers to the good inclination. "And behold it was very good," this is the evil inclination. And is the evil inclination very good? (How are both inclinations considered "very good?") If it were not for the evil inclination a person would not build a house (procreate), he would not do business . . . and thus did King Solomon say, 'And I saw that all labor and all skillful work is the result of man's jealousy with his neighbor' " (*Koheles* 4:4), (*Bereishis Rabbah* 9:9).

The *Etz Yosef* (ibid) explains that all the labor and skillful work in this world comes about through the jealousy of individuals to achieve more than their neighbor, and jealousy and desire are designs of the evil inclination. Therefore, this inclination is called "evil" even though there are many times when it causes things to transpire which are, "very good." This explanation helps us understand a very puzzling verse in the Torah, "And Hashem said in His Heart, I will not continue to curse the ground because of man since the inclination of man is evil from his youth" (*Bereishis* 8:21). What difference does it make *when* man's inclination becomes evil? What would be the difference if man's inclination became evil when he matured? Wouldn't there still be reason for Hashem not to curse the earth because of man? The fact of the matter is that since man has an evil inclination it is exceedingly difficult for him to rule over it, therefore Hashem should forgive him and not curse the earth irrespective of when this evil inclination became empowered. However, according to what our Sages taught — we can say that when the Torah states, "For the inclination of man is evil from his youth," the Torah means that *only* from his youth is his inclination evil. When he is young, immature, carefree and careless, his evil inclination does not produce any good. However, once he matures into adulthood, his evil inclination is not exclusively evil, at times it can be "very good." For it is the evil inclination that spurs him on to procreate, do business and engage in all types of endeavors which are necessary for society to function properly. If this is so, why do we call jealousy and desire designs of the evil inclination and the absence of these traits we attribute to the good inclination?

We refer to it in this manner based on its *primary thought* and *intent* and not according to the *deed* which is the end result. The Torah tells us, "And every formation of the thoughts of his (man's) heart was only for evil" (*Bereishis* 6:5). While jealousy and desire are in the heart, they are being nurtured and nourished by the evil inclination whose intent is negative. Therefore, even after a person translates this thought into a positive deed — to the extent that it is called "very good" — the source from which it came, the place which bore it and nurtured it does not cease to be evil, neither in its foundation nor in its make up.

We can now understand why an idol worshipper is called "uncircumcised" (ערל), even if for some reason he has undergone circumcision. The Torah has commanded *us* to enter into the Covenant of Circumcision. This individual has no such commandment and his act — for whatever reason he undertakes it — is not done לשם מצוה, for the sake of the *Mitzvah*. Thus, it remains a physical act without any spiritual (Torah) ramification. Similarly, a Jew who is uncircumcised is called a *Mahul* (circumcised) because we follow the primary thought and intent and not the deed.

The case in the Talmud where the uncircumcised Jew is called an ערל deals with a person whose brothers died in the course of circumcision — thus, since it is a danger for him to become circumcised, he is exempt from this *mitzvah*. But, his primary thought and intent is that he wants to enter into this Covenant, although he is unable to carry out the deed and achieve the final result due to circumstances beyond his control.

The *Torah Temimah* explains that Moshe called the evil inclination a foreskin (ערל) because just as the physical foreskin is attached to the body, so too, does the evil inclination cling to us in the realm of spirituality.

As you enter your son into this dual Covenant today and involve him in his very first *mitzvah*, may you merit to involve him further in Torah, and lead him to the *Chuppah* and good deeds. Mazel Tov.

(Based in part on *Panim Chadashos BaTorah*, by Rav Ben Tzion Firer).

פרשת ראה
Parshas Re'eh

_____ Rabbi Jay Marcus_

*P*ARSHAS *RE'EH* IS ONE OF THE *PARSHIYOS* OF THE TORAH THAT CONTAIN THE *mitzvos* of the *Moadim* or *Shalosh Regalim,* the Three Pilgrimage Festivals. The very first *Yom Tov* which marks the beginning of the Jewish year is *Chag Ha'Pesach.* To commemorate our deliverance from Egypt, each Jew is commanded to offer a *Korban Pesach* or Passover offering. This sacrifice is so important that the Torah even makes special allowances if one is unable to bring the *Korban Pesach* at the designated time. Unlike any other *mitzvah*, the opportunity to bring a *Pesach Sheini* one month later is provided. The severity of failing to bring the *Korban Pesach* is also obvious from the punishment dictated by the Torah. The Torah informs us that the punishment for this transgression is *Kares,* being spiritually cut off before one's time. It is fascinating to note that there is only one other positive commandment (מצות עשה) in the Torah that also carries the punishment of *Kares* if one fails to fulfill it — *Bris Milah.*

The *Shulchan Aruch, Yoreh Deiah,* Section 260 begins the laws of *Bris Milah* with the following *Halachah*: There is a positive commandment for a father to circumcise his son and this *mitzvah* is greater than all other positive commandments. The *Shach*, commenting on the statement that *Milah* is greater than other positive commandments, tells us that the reason is because it is a punishable by *Kares* if one grows up and fails to circumcise himself. One may wonder why is *Milah* singled out? *Korban*

_____

Rabbi Marcus is rav of the Young Israel of Staten Island, New York.

Pesach also carries the punishment of *Kares* so what is the connection between these two *Mitzvos Aseh*?

The *Halachah* teaches us that one of the requirements to be able to eat the *Korban Pesach* is that you must be circumcised — כל ערל לא יאכל בו (*Shemos* 12:48). To bring the *Korban Pesach* you must have undergone a *Bris Milah*, otherwise you are excluded. Obviously, *Bris Milah* which enables you to offer the *Pesach* seemingly has the greater significance. Why then does this link between the *Bris* and *Korban Pesach* exist? What message does it convey? It is possible that *Bris Milah* and *Korban Pesach* represent the same ideal and value. *Bris* signifies it on the *individual* level and *Korban Pesach* on the *national* level.

For an individual Jewish male the *Bris* represents his covenant with G-d personally, while the *Korban Pesach* represents the individual joining *Am Yisrael* communally. Prior to joining the communal *Am Yisrael* with his offering, every male has the responsibility to personally enter the *Bris shel Avraham Avinu.* This is the בדמיך חיי בדמיך חיי referred to in *Yechezkel* and recited aloud at every *Bris Milah* — the intermingling of דם מילה, the blood of *Bris Milah* and דם פסח, the blood of the *Korban Pesach* at the very first *Korban Pesach* offered in Egypt.

May the parents of the newborn who has just fulfilled the first *personal* aspect of his commitment as a Jew be *zocheh* to raise him to become a true *ben Torah* and assume his *communal* responsibility as well.

פרשת שפטים
Parshas Shoftim
— for a Pidyon Haben

_____ *Rabbi Harry Levinson*

THE CEREMONY OF *"PIDYON HABEN"* IS ONE OF THE MOST UNIQUE RITUALS OF our people. On a date 30 days after the birth of a first born son to Jewish parents who are neither *Kohanim* or Levites (nor is the mother a daughter of a *Kohen* or Levite), a very joyous feast is arranged by the parents of this child. At that time, the child is "redeemed" by the father from the *Kohen* (who is usually chosen by the child's parents to officiate at this event) for five silver coins containing a total of 3.56 ounces of silver (which in the United States is customarily five silver dollars) and this constitutes the *"Pidyon Haben,"* literally, the "redemption of the son." The fact is that *"Pidyon Haben"* is one of the many offerings we are required to give to the *Kohanim* (*"Matnos Kehunah"*).

In this week's *parshah* — Shoftim — the Torah describes the various offerings to be given the *Kohanim*. In discussing the *"Matnos Kehunah,"* the Torah states: "He [the tribe of Levi (which includes the *Kohanim*)] shall not have an inheritance [in Eretz Yisrael] among his brothers; Hashem is his inheritance as He [Hashem] has spoken to him" (*Devarim* 18:2). The *Yalkut Shimoni* (Chapter 915) explains this with a parable: The Chief Judge of a Jewish Court had many sons all of whom were ignorant in Torah studies (עמי ארץ), with the exception of his eldest son who was a Torah scholar (*"ben Torah"*). The Chief Judge bequeathed in writing a portion of

_____

Rabbi Levinson is an attorney who lives in Monsey, New York and practices in New York City.

his estate to each of his sons, but not the eldest one. He then said to his father: "You bequeathed to each of my brothers a portion of your estate, yet you failed to bequeath anything to me." The father replied: "It is sufficient that you will take over my position as Chief Judge of the Court." In the same way, continues the *Yalkut Shimoni*, the tribe of Levi said to Hashem: "You have written out a gift of a portion of Eretz Yisrael to each of the other tribes, while to our tribe You have not given this gift." And Hashem responded: "To the tribe of Levi it is sufficient that you are inheriting My position (that is, the service in the *Beis Hamikdash* and the study and dissemination of Torah)."

The *Ksav Sofer* explains why the tribe of Levi did not receive a portion of Eretz Yisrael. He points out that the tribe of Levi was chosen by Hashem for the service in the *Beis Hamikdash* and for the study and transmission of Torah. If they would have also received a portion of Eretz Yisrael like the other tribes, they would have developed the trait of arrogance and superiority vis-a-vis the rest of *Am Yisrael*. However, the service of Hashem and the study and transmission of Torah can **only** be properly effected by those who possess humility. Thus, in order to instill the attribute of humility in the tribe of Levi, Hashem did not give them a portion of Eretz Yisrael but instead made them dependent for their livelihood upon the "*Matnos Kehunah*" to be given to them by their fellow Jews.

This emphasis on humility which we find with regard to the tribe of Levi, the teachers of Torah and the ones who conducted the service of Hashem in the *Beis Hamikdash*, can also be observed with respect to the Jewish kings, the temporal leader of *Am Yisrael*. The Torah states in this week's *parshah* that the Jewish king should write a *Sefer Torah* that he shall study in order that he will perform all of the Torah commandments. The Torah then adds "in order that he [the Jewish king] shall not raise his heart [become haughty] over his brothers" (17:20). *Ramban* explains this verse by pointing out that the Torah is indicating the serious perils of the sin of haughtiness and arrogance, even for a king and certainly for ordinary persons who are not royalty. The *Ramban* further states that the trait of arrogance is totally despicable to Hashem even when it is possessed by a king.

The message of "*Pidyon Haben*" is similar to the Torah's teaching regarding the tribe of Levi and the Jewish king, namely, that of humility. Parents who just had the good fortune to have a first born son and the privilege to perform the great *mitzvah* of *Bris Milah* could, in their great feelings of euphoria, develop an attitude of arrogance. As we have explained, this would seriously and adversely impair their relationship with Hashem and their ability to properly perform *mitzvos*. Thus, the Torah says to the parents: "Your beloved son does not really belong to you — you have to redeem him from the *Kohen* and only then does your son belong to you." In this way, the parents realize that their most prized possession, their first born son, is in all respects a gift of Hashem and so, in fact, are all of their other worldly possessions. This realization creates the appropriate mindset of humility in the parents' relationship to Hashem and enables them to properly perform their obligations as Torah Jews and to transmit these values to their children.

As a result, if we perform the *mitzvah* of "*Pidyon Haben*" in this manner, then, in the words of the Prophet Yeshayahu in this week's *Haftorah*, we will merit to see the fulfillment of the prophecy that "We shall see [with our own eyes] the return to Zion" as part of the Great Redemption and the rebuilding of the *Beis Hamikdash*.

פרשת כי תצא
Parshas Ki Seitzei

_____ *Rabbi Yitzchok Adlerstein*

THE OPENING LINES OF THE *PARSHAH* HOLD SIGNIFICANT PROMISE FOR US. There seems to be the possibility of giving in to various temptations that the Torah expects us to avoid.

And why not? After all, the Torah provides a similar license regarding יפת תאר, the beautiful captive woman. According to *Chazal*, the Torah realized that many men would not be able to resist the temptation of the women they would encounter in wartime. It, therefore, created a special provision for these soldiers to legally marry them after a mandatory cooling-off period. Effectively, the Torah seems to place a very big *hechsher* on some very *treif* unions. Better to have people act within the law than to have them violate it, the law seems to propose.

So can I have that cheeseburger, if getting a whiff of one makes me salivate uncontrollably? Not quite, said Rav Chatzkel Abramsky, *zt"l.* There is a world of difference between the two situations. The Torah teaches us to deal with temptation by avoiding it. If I know that I have a weakness for something illicit, the Torah takes it for granted that I will police myself. I am expected to know my vulnerabilities, and to make sure that I deal with them appropriately. If I know that the *yetzer hara* often gets the best of me under certain circumstances, the Torah expects me to avoid those circumstances!

Warfare, though, leaves me no option. If I discover that the life of a

_____

Rabbi Adlerstein is director of the Jewish Studies Institute of the Yeshiva of Los Angeles in Los Angeles, California.

soldier opens up a Pandora's box of temptations, I do not have the option of resigning my commission. The Torah demands my participation in the war effort, like it or not. I have no recourse to the flight and escape that the Torah usually calls for.

On the other hand, if cheeseburgers drive me mad with desire when I pass a MacDonalds, then I should take another route home. Or, I should always pass by in the company of a friend who is vegetarian, who will remind me of my Torah obligation if he sees me losing my resolve. The Torah expects us to compensate for our personal weaknesses through great self-awareness, honesty, and barrier-building.

We certainly keep these ideas in mind at the birth of a new child. Much of parenting is concerned with exposing our children to things that are wholesome and stimulating. A great deal concerns the other side of the coin — keeping them away from experiences that we believe will harm their progress as Torah-true Jews.

But like the soldier on the battlefield, we cannot control everything. Parents can go only so far. Some things are beyond us . . .

When Hashem called upon our founding father Avraham to submit to *Bris Milah,* He told him that by fulfilling this *mitzvah,* our patriarch would become *tamim,* perfected. Rashi, citing *Nedarim 32b,* amplifies the idea. Till now, says G-d, you have perfected yourself with virtually every part of your body. However, five organs have escaped you: the eyes, ears, and sexual organ. Observe this *mitzvah,* and you will be master of these five as well. And to mark this triumph, we will add the letter *heh* — the numerical equivalent of five — to Avram, changing your name to Avraham.

How are these five different? Precisely because we have limited mastery of them. We control only so much of our immediate environment. We do our best, hopefully, but there is no predicting what will enter our visual field a minute from now, or what sounds will enter our ears that only wish to listen to holiness, to *kedushah.* Hashem tells us that we must do ours. Then, if we practice *Milah,* we can rely on Him to do the rest.

This is very reassuring as we bring a new child into the community. We desperately want to do the right thing, but at the same time recognize how much can go wrong. *Bris Milah* reassures us. It reminds us that we are in partnership with G-d. We do what is humanly possible, and He takes up the slack.

Another insight from the *parshah* indicates how hard we must try to fulfill our side of the bargain. Following on the heels of the יפת תאר section is the description of the incorrigible son, the בן סורר ומורה. This young person is executed in anticipation of the evil he will certainly commit. *Chazal* see a connection between these sections: One whose appetite cannot be controlled, one who deludes himself into thinking that the object of his infatuation will one day become a fine Jewish mother — such a person will father a בן סורר ומורה.

A fine thought, says the *Shem M'Shmuel*. But the two sections do not quite dovetail. They are separated from each other by the *parshah* of inheritance, specifying a double portion for the *bechor*, the firstborn. If the Torah meant to predict what the offspring of the יפת תאר would grow to become, then בן סורר ומורה should have followed directly.

On second thought, offers the *Shem M'Shmuel*, the *bechor* section elegantly fits within the development of this theme. The firstborn receives an enhanced inheritance — because he is first! The Torah means to underscore how important **beginnings** are to us. The hapless בן סורר ומורה struck out twice; both times were at crucial **beginnings.** His parents' marriage started off on the wrong foot. It was born of lust and desire, rather than commitment to shared values. His own adulthood began with a gluttonous revelry in stolen food and drink.

If poor beginnings predict spiritual failing, surely the opposite is part of the recipe for success. *Bris Milah* is important for binding us to our glorious past. But we should also remember that it marks the beginning of the education of this child. We want so much for him to grow to be a proud, observant Jew. To succeed, all our hopes and aspirations for him, all our fervently wished *berachos,* and all our determination to provide him with the wherewithal to become a *talmid chacham* and true servant of G-d — all these should be in place now, at the beginning.

It is an awesome, daunting task. But the *parshah* reassures us. We must do ours, and Hashem will certainly do His.

פרשת כי תבוא
Parshas Ki Savo

Rabbi Jeffrey Bienenfeld

PARSHAS KI SAVO OPENS WITH THE COMMANDMENT TO THE CHILDREN OF Israel obliging them to bring their first fruits to Jerusalem. This _mitzvah_ of _Bikurim_ was accompanied by a moving declaration of gratitude which ended with the following verse: ועתה הנה הבאתי את ראשית פרי האדמה אשר נתתה לי ה' — "And now, behold, I have brought the first fruit of the ground which You, Hashem, have given me" (_Devarim_ 26:10).

On the opening three words of this verse, ועתה הנה הבאתי, the _Sifre_ offers the following terse commentary: "ועתה, _and now_, מיד — implying, _immediately_; הנה, _behold_ — בשמחה, connoting _joy_; הבאתי, _I brought_, משלי — implying, _of my own._"

The author of the _Divrei Shaarei Chayim_ sees in this explanation a paradigm for the proper fulfillment of any _mitzvah_. If a _mitzvah_ is to be performed in an exemplary fashion, its observance must reflect three basic elements:

(1) The _mitzvah_ should be done at once, מיד, without delay. One should never take the attitude that one can postpone doing the Will of Hashem until a more convenient time.

(2) One should delight in the opportunity to do a _mitzvah_ and not consider its obligation a burden. The emotion surrounding a _mitzvah_ should be one of _simcha_.

(3) One should never justify not committing oneself to _mitzvah_ observance by claiming a lack of time or money, or the inability to meet the

Rabbi Bienenfeld is rav of the Young Israel of St. Louis, Missouri.

religious challenge of obeying G-d's command. If, as the *Sifre* says, it is משלי, of one's own, then whatever you can contribute — at the present moment — to a given *mitzvah* performance is sufficient no matter the circumstances.

If the *mitzvah* of *Bikurim* can serve as a model for the performance of all *mitzvos*, then the very same can be said for the *mitzvah* of *Bris Milah*. The popular refrain and prayer proclaimed by the assembled at a *Bris* makes the point quite clearly: כשם שנכנס לברית כן יכנס לתורה ולחפה ולמעשים טובים — "In the same fashion that this child was introduced into the Covenant, may he be so initiated into the study of Torah, to the marriage canopy, and to a life of good deeds."

Indeed, the manner in which this child is initiated into the Covenant reflects the very same three-fold commitment that marked the bringing of the *Bikurim*. First, the parents do not wait or hesitate to perform the *mitzvah* at its appropriate time. As soon as the eighth day arrives, mother and father are eager to obey G-d's command. Second, the simple fact that every *Bris* is combined with a joyous *seudas mitzvah,* a festive meal, speaks to the *simcha* and gratitude that parents feel in celebrating the *Bris* of their son. And finally, it matters little what the economic or social circumstances of the parents might be. Nor does it matter the level of religiosity or Jewish knowledge they have achieved. The *mitzvah* can be performed with whatever they have — materially and religiously — at that moment. And this first *mitzvah* of their newborn son is as cherished and esteemed as that of the *Bikurim.* Indeed, every mother and father who bring their son into the Convenant of *Bris Milah,* are expressing the exact same dedication as did the Jewish farmer of old when he brought his first fruit: "ועתה הנה הבאתי...". Cradling their new-born son, the parents stand before the Al-mighty and also proudly declare: "And now, behold, we have brought (our son to You)."

Our *berachah* to the רך הנמול, to the newly circumcised baby, today is that just as this first *mitzvah* in your life was performed with זריזות, alacrity with *simcha* and with whatever your parents possessed, so too, may your future be similarly blessed. As you grow and enter the world of Torah, of marriage and of good deeds, may these fundamental pillars of Jewish life be fulfilled in the same beautiful fashion that this *Bris* was performed this morning: with genuine eagerness, with joy and gladness, and with all the wonderful talents and gifts that Hashem, in His Goodness, has bestowed upon you. Mazel Tov!

פרשת נצבים
Parshas Netzavim

_____ _Rabbi Nosson Fromowitz_

A S ROSH HASHANAH RAPIDLY APPROACHES AND WE PREPARE FOR THE DAY OF Judgment we should use every opportunity and occasion as a time for reflection and introspection.

The birth of a male child and the subsequent _mitzvos_ that follow give us an opportunity to reflect upon the special nature of the Jewish people's relationship with Hashem. On the eighth day after the birth of a male, the father is commanded to circumcise his son. At the moment that the circumcision takes place the father makes the blessing, "and has commanded us to bring him into the covenant of Abraham, our forefather."

This _mitzvah of Bris Milah_ marks the entry of the child into the special covenant that G-d has with His people. As the Torah describes in _Bereishis_ 17:11, ונמלתם את בשר ערלתכם והיה לאות ברית ביני וביניכם — "And you will circumcise the flesh of your foreskin and it will be a covenant between Me and you." This is not merely a _mitzvah_ we must perform, but rather a sign of the child's entry into this special relationship with our Creator and the rest of _Klal Yisrael._

In _Parshas Netzavim_ the Torah gives us a special insight into the nature of this relationship.

Moshe _Rabbeinu_ on the day before his departure from this world gathers all of the Jewish people to give them his final charge and to define for all time the covenant between G-d and His people. In so doing, we find

_____

Rabbi Fromowitz is executive director of the Yeshiva of Spring Valley in Monsey, New York.

inconsistency in Moshe's words. He begins, אתם נצבים היום כלכם — "You are standing here today, all of you" (Devarim 29:9),which is in a plural form. He continues, למען הקים אתך היום לו לעם והוא יהיה לך לאלקים — "in order that He establish you today as a nation to Him and He will be a G-d to you" (v. 12), in the singular form and then again in the next verse it switches to the plural form: ולא אתכם לבדכם אנכי כרת את הברית הזאת — "and not with you alone do I seal this covenant" but with all future generations.

What is it that the Torah is teaching us through this obvious shift in form?

Our *Chazal* tell us that Moshe *Rabbeinu* was at that moment defining the essence and very nature of the covenant *Am Yisrael* has with G-d. When *Bnai Yisrael* gathered to hear the words of Moshe, they came as a mass of individuals. Each one had his own individual commitment and relationship. When Moshe *Rabbeinu* bonded them together, they were no longer כל איש ישראל, "every member of Israel" (v. 9). They gathered למען הקים אתך היום לו לעם, "in order to establish you as a nation" (v. 12). The very nature of the covenant was to bind *Am Yisroel* with Hashem. They were no longer accepting the Torah as separate and disparate individuals but as a new entity, a unified body. The significance of this single body is that future generations are bound by this covenant.

As a member born to *Klal Yisrael* one is automatically bound by their commitments, in the same manner that a soldier is obligated to obey the orders of his General.

The Torah then shifts to the plural to let us know ולא אתכם לבדכם אנכי כרת את הברית הזאת — it is *not* with you (plural) as individuals that the covenant is made but even ואת אשר איננו פה עמנו היום, "those who are not present with us today" nevertheless, are bound by the commitment of the unified entity called *Am Yisrael.*

When a child enters the covenant of Avraham *Avinu* through the *Bris Milah,* he is entering the fold of *Am Yisrael* and is thereby defining for all of us the special nature of the relationship between ourselves as Jews and between us and Hashem.

When a segment of Jews or even an individual Jew who is a member of the singular entity of *Am Yisrael* is in pain, we must feel that pain and attempt to alleviate it. The great leaders of our people were always acutely aware of the plight of *every* Jew and were pained by the suffering of even a single individual. Responsibility for each other's spiritual and physical well-being is commensurate with our feeling of being part of this singular being.

A story is told of the famous Mirrer Yeshiva that was miraculously saved from the inferno of the Holocaust by escaping to Shanghai, China. During the war the Yeshiva continued to function, albeit in somewhat crowded quarters in a local synagogue. It was shortly before the *Yomim Noraim,* "Days of Awe," when a group of students decided to learn in the *Ezras Nashim,* the women's gallery.

The Rosh Yeshiva, Rav Chaim Shmuelevitz, was told of the students' seemingly innocent intention. His reaction was immediate and powerful, "*Chas v'shalom,* G-d forbid, how can one separate himself from the *tzibbur,* community? G-d forbid that they be judged apart from the rest of us. The power of the community of *Klal Yisrael* and the individual's commitment to that entity is our greatest source of strength."

At the time of this celebration, let us use this occasion to commit ourselves to feeling the special bond that the *Bris* represents to us as a people.

פרשת וילך
Parshas Vayeilech

_____ *Rabbi Benjamin Yudin*

PARSHAS *VAYEILECH* HAS THE DISTINCTION OF BEING THE SHORTEST *PARSHAH* IN the Torah. Yet, it contains the last *mitzvah* of the Torah (according to the Rambam) — to write a *sefer Torah,* as well as the promise to the Jewish nation, that Torah will never be forgotten from the mouth of its offspring (*Devarim* 31:19-21).

It is interesting to note, that the *mitzvah* of *Milah* is not only to place a permanent physical representation of the close intimate relationship between Hashem and His people, on the body of a Jew, but *Milah* prepares and enables the Jewish male to absorb, master and become one with the Torah. The Talmud *Pesachim* (54a) teaches "seven things were created in the spiritual world before the physical world was created" and the first one is Torah. The Torah, the Ramban teaches in his introduction to his commentary on the Torah, is all the 'names' or essence of Hashem Himself. Understandably, the Torah is our holiest object, and can only be studied and mastered by one who is himself holy. The *Bris* is called "*bris kodesh,*" the holy covenant, as we elevate the baby to a higher spiritual level, enabling him to receive the higher divine frequency.

The *Daas Zekanim M'Baalei HaTosfos* at the beginning of *Parshas Mishpatim* cites the story of Onkelos, the famous translator/commentator of the Torah. He was the nephew of the Roman Caeser who, sensing an emptiness and void in his life of higher meaning and purpose, asked the scholars of Israel to teach him Torah. They refused, saying that one who is

_____
Rabbi Yudin is rav of Shomrei Torah Orthodox Congregation of Fair Lawn, Fair Lawn, New Jersey.

⮬ ENTERING THE COVENANT

not circumcised may not master Torah. He underwent circumcision and became a great Torah scholar. His uncle was most distressed that he underwent circumcision, but Onkelos cited the verse from *Tehillim* (147: 19,20), "He relates His word to Jacob, (one circumcised as Jacob), His statutes and judgments to Israel. He did not do so for any other nation."

The strong connection between *Milah* and studying Torah may be seen from the following interesting *halachah.* If, for whatever reason, the father of the baby cannot be present at the *Bris,* who will recite the blessing of להכניסו בבריתו של אברהם אבינו — "to bring him into the Covenant of Abraham our father"? Rabbi Akiva Eiger *zt"l,* in his responsa (42) cites the *Ollelos Ephraim* (387) that *milah* of the foreskin accomplishes "*milas halev*" — circumcising the heart, preparing and enabling the Jewish male to acquire and absorb the study of Torah. Thus, the *Levush* in his commentary on the *Shulchan Aruch* (265) understands the *berachah* of להכניסו to be one of preparing the child for the study of Torah. Therefore, reasons Rabbi Akiva Eiger, the primary responsibility to teach the child Torah is on the father. However, the Torah includes in this *mitzvah* the grandfather as well, as we are taught, "And make them known to your children and your children's children" (*Devarim* 4:9). There is a special privilege and obligation on the grandfather to transmit the *mesorah,* holy tradition, to the subsequent generations. Consequently, in the absence of the father, if the grandfather is present, he recites this special *berachah.*

Finally, the Talmud in *Niddah* (30b) states that in addition to teaching the child Torah in the womb, an oath is administered to the baby prior to birth: "Be a righteous individual and not one who does evil. Even if all around you shall assess you as being a righteous person, know there is always room for improvement, and you are deficient and not yet perfect. Know that Hashem is pure (holy) and those who are privileged to serve Him are pure (holy), and your soul is pure (holy)."

Today, at the *Bris Kodesh* we have elevated the sanctity and potential of this baby to acquire more holiness throughout his life. May he emulate the noble character of his parents and grandparents, bring honor to the name that he carries, and be a source of *nachas* to his family, community and all of Israel.

פרשת האזינו
Parshas Ha'azinu

_____ *Rabbi David Stavsky*

No WORDS ARE MORE MEANINGFUL FOR US TODAY, AS WE CELEBRATE THE *simcha* of a *Bris* than the words in this week's *parshah*: זכר ימות עולם בינו שנות דור ודור — "Remember the days of old, understand the years of generation after generation" (*Devarim* 32:7). What is this charge made by Moshe *Rabbeinu* as he bids farewell to his people? What is this mandate to "understand the years of generation after generation?"

I submit that we must understand that we are part of an eternal golden chain, where each link is a generation unto itself. Every link is precious and has been forged through the fires of faith.

As we examine the word דור — "generation," we realize how essential and fundamental that word is in Judaism. We are constantly reminded of generations past.

On Pesach night we say, בכל דור ודור חייב אדם וכו' — "In every generation each Jew should regard himself as though he personally went out of Egypt."

In a month, please G-d, we will celebrate the Succos holiday and we are instructed to build a *succah*, למען ידעו דרתיכם כי בסכות הושבתי את בני ישראל — "So the generations will know that I have caused the Children of Israel to dwell in booths" (*Vayikra* 23:43).

These examples from our *Mesorah* help us understand the concept that we do not live in the existential moment of time, but rather we are part of a past, present and future.

_____

Rabbi Stavsky is rav of Congregation Beth Jacob, Columbus, Ohio.

In the אשרי prayer, which we recite daily, we say דור לדור ישבח מעשיך וגבורתך יגידו — "From generation to generation, they will praise Your deeds and will speak of Your mighty acts." What the Psalmist has in mind is that every generation, through its own cognition, realizes the wonders of G-d; that there is a Supreme Being. It is incumbent upon the children of that generation to transmit their knowledge of His deeds to the following generation.

As we celebrate and welcome the newborn infant into the convenental community of Hashem, we say to him, "In your hands, lies not only the legacy of our past, but the destiny of our future. Know where you came from (previous generations — your *zayde,* your *buba*) and that you are a most important link in creating future generations of loyal Jews."

Furthermore, "know my precious child, that the word "שנות" does not only mean "years," it also means "change" (לשנות). In your hands, lies the choice of changing the Jewish world, to be a greater, stronger and more committed Jewish world."

דור לדור יגידו — the word יגידו is written in the future tense. This is to teach you, my dear child, not to be satisfied with simply inheriting the past, but rather perpetuating a greater future.

Mazel Tov to the entire family.

פרשת וזאת הברכה
Vezos Haberachah

_____ *Rabbi Elazar Muskin*

ON THE EVE OF SIMCHAS TORAH, MANY SYNAGOC TES AUCTION THE THREE major honors of the day, with proceeds benefiting the synagogue or other Jewish institutions. Two honors, *Chassan Torah* (for the one called to the final reading in *Devarim*) and *Chassan Bereishis* (for the one called to the first reading in *Bereishis*), usually receive the highest bids, while the third, כל הנערים (supervising the blessing of all minor children as a *talis* is held over their heads while he receives the next to the last *aliya* in *Vezos Haberachah*) can be a close second.

One year, however, the auction for כל הנערים in my synagogue was unusually competitive. When finally over, I asked the man who fiercely bid the highest why he vied for this honor.

Surprised by my question, he replied as if it were self-evident: "The one who supervises scores of little children crowded under the *talis*, reciting the same blessing Jacob uttered over his grandchildren, is himself guaranteed Jewish grandchildren. Could I want less for myself?"

Those words come to me again and again whenever I contemplate the unique Torah portion, *Vezos Haberachah*, which is the only *parshah* not identified with a specific Shabbos. Rather, it is reserved for the joyous Simchas Torah holiday with its unique כל הנערים ceremony and as such deserves close analysis.

The Talmud in *Sukkah* 42a referring to *Vezos Haberachah*, provides a provocative comment, stating: "Our Rabbis taught: A minor who is able to

_____

Rabbi Muskin is rav of the Young Israel of Century City in Los Angeles, California.

speak, his father must teach him Torah. . . What could be meant by Torah? Rav Hamnuna replied, the Scriptural verse, תורה צוה לנו משה מורשה קהלת יעקב — *Moses commanded us a law, an inheritance of the congregation of Jacob"* (*Devarim* 33:4).

Rabbi Baruch Halevi Epstein, an early 20th century commentator, questions why the Talmud chose this particular passage as the first Torah verse that a parent must teach a child. Rabbi Epstein suggests that by referring to Torah as a *"Morasha,"* an inheritance of all Jews, young and old alike, it rejects the notion that only mature adults are obligated to observe Torah. An inheritance is age blind, and so, too, is the Torah.

The word *"Morasha,"* however, may contain another dimension. An early 19th century German scholar, the *Ksav V'Kabblah,* notes that the usual word for inheritance is *"Yerusha,"* not *"Morasha."* In fact, *"Morasha"* is best translated as "a possession" rather than "an inheritance." The difference is crucial. One receives an inheritance without individual effort, but one attains a possession through personal exertion. Torah, in other words, requires personal exertion, rather than effortless lineage. The only way to become fluent in Torah is to work at studying Torah.

Finally, the 19th century scholar, *Kesav Sofer,* remarks that, מורשה קהלת יעקב ("a possession of the congregation of Jacob"), teaches that no Jew is an island unto himself. No Jew can observe **all** of the *mitzvos* of the Torah, for the 613 commandments do not all apply to any one person. Some only apply to *Kohanim,* others to *Levi'im,* some to women, while others only to those who live in Israel. It is only as a part of a *Kehilla,* the congregation of Israel, that we can become complete Jews.

Certainly these lessons are themes that the beautiful כל הנערים ceremony emphasize. First, each child has a right to Torah, it is an inheritance that comes with birth.

Second, כל הנערים suggests that Torah requires effort. Neither children nor adults will acquire knowledge unless they work at studying Torah. If they put in the effort, they will be rewarded with the greatest gift — the Torah itself.

And, finally, we must appreciate that a Jewish life must include the community of fellow Jews, the קהלת יעקב. The little children are blessed as part of an entire group — part of a future community — because Torah cannot be lived in isolation. Instead, our blessing emphasizes the need for everyone to be involved with the Jewish community, for only together do we comprise the *Kehillas Yaakov* that both *Vezos Haberachah* and Simchas Torah celebrate.

May the רך הנמול join the כל הנערים and utilize his priceless inheritance of Torah. We hope and pray that as he grows and develops he will expend the necessary efforts to be an עמל בתורה — to toil in Torah and *mitzvos* and be a source of *nachas* to his family and the entire Jewish community.

Yamim Tovim

ראש השנה
Rosh Hashanah

_____ *Rabbi Ralph Pelcovitz*

TIMING IS ALL IMPORTANT WHEN IT COMES TO A *BRIS MILAH*. THE TORAH ordained that this ritual be performed on the eighth day after the birth of a male child, and this timing is so important that the procedure is even דוחה שבת — it overrides the strictures of Shabbos! Not only is the day important, but even the time of day, which is why, under normal circumstances, the *halachah* demands that we perform this *mitzvah* as early as possible on the eighth day.

However, there are times when we postpone the performance of this *mitzvah,* even on the eighth day. Such is the case when a *Bris* is scheduled to be held on Rosh Hashanah; in that situation the law is that we should perform this great *mitzvah* immediately *before* the sounding of the *shofar.* The reason given is a bit unusual for it is built upon the phraseology of one of the *Selichos,* which reads: זכור ברית אברהם ועקדת יצחק — "Remember (oh G-d) the Covenant of Abraham (circumcision) and the binding of Isaac," which indicates that the *Bris* should *precede* the *Akeidah,* which we memorialize by sounding the *shofar.*

The *halachah* seems to be built on a firm foundation, but one might argue that we are begging the question. Why, indeed, is the covenantal act of *Bris Milah* given preference to the reminder of the *Akeidah* (the binding of Isaac), which plays such a prominent role in the Rosh Hashanah service?

_____
Rabbi Pelcovitz is rabbi emeritus of Congregation Kneseth Israel, Far Rockaway, New York.

The *Akeidah* represents the willingness of Avraham to fulfill G-d's will, even if it meant giving up the life of his child. This was the ultimate act of קדוש השם — "the sanctification of G-d's Name." It represented the supreme sacrifice of offering one's son as a *korban*. It is interesting to note that the performance of the *mitzvah* of *Bris Milah* is also compared to the offering of a *korban* on the altar. The phraseology used in the *Aruch HaShulchan (Yoreh Deiah 265)* is, "The lap of the *sandek* is comparable to an altar, and the infant being circumcised is compared to a *korban* (offering)." We now see that there is a strong link between *Bris Milah* and the *Akeidah*. The question, however, remains as to why we should give precedence to the former over the latter.

In Judaism, there is a basic concept called *mesiras nefesh*, meaning total commitment on the part of an individual to fulfill the will of Hashem or to sacrifice oneself on behalf of another. When a Jew is committed to his faith, he is prepared even to offer his life on behalf of that faith. Through the ages, Jews have been willing to be executed and burned at the stake rather than to deny their belief in G-d and in the Torah.

This special willingness can be traced to the act of Avraham and Yitzchak when the father brought his son as a sacrifice, and the son consented to be offered as a קרבן לה'. It is this act which we commemorate every Rosh Hashanah when we sound the *shofar*, for the *shofar* is symbolic of the ram which was offered in the place of Yitzchak. The symbolism of the *shofar*, the ram's horn, is not only to remember the *Akeidah*, but also to remind us of the *shofar* sounded at Sinai when the Torah was given, as well as being symbolic of the great *shofar* which will be sounded at the time of our total and final redemption.

However, as important and significant as the *shofar* is, even greater is the lesson of *Bris Milah*, the sign of the Covenant. Whereas the *Akeidah* represents the willingness, if need be, to *die* for the sanctification of G-d's name, the *Bris Milah* represents the willingness to *live* one's life in a manner which fulfills the Covenant entered into by Avraham and his descendants. It is more difficult to live a life of Torah and *Mitzvos* for many years, under all circumstances, than to be willing to die על קדוש השם. That is why ברית אברהם takes precedence over the *Akeidah* of Yitzchak.

Buttressing this thought, it is fitting to quote the *Yerushalmi*, which explains a phrase in the Torah regarding Rosh Hashanah. In *Parshas Pinchas (Bamidbar 29:2)*, regarding the offering brought on the first day of the seventh month, the expression used is: ועשיתם עולה — "And you shall *make* an elevation offering." The *Yerushalmi* comments, "Why regarding all *korbonos,* it is written: והקרבתם — "And you shall offer," while here (regarding the Rosh Hashanah offering) it is written: ועשיתם — "And you shall make?"

The answer is that, on Rosh Hashanah when you stand before G-d to be judged and are vindicated, it is considered as though you have just been created as a new person.

On Rosh Hashanah, when we are judged and found to be meritorious and worthy of G-d's blessing, we have *remade ourselves.* How interesting it is that the character of Rosh Hashanah is such that each one of us is, as it were, reborn, and we bring ourselves as an offering to G-d, just as we bring this child as a *korban* at the time of his *Bris Milah.*

We can now appreciate the relationship between a *Bris Milah* and Rosh Hashanah, and we can also understand more fully the sequence of the penitential prayer: זכור ברית אברהם ועקדת יצחק —"Remember the Covenant of Abraham and the binding of Isaac." We give precedence to the *Bris,* the convenant, over the *Akeidah* because our commitment to *live* a covenantal life, based on Torah, is a greater challenge than a Jew's willingness to give up his life for Hashem.

May this child, whose *Bris* was performed on Rosh Hashanah, merit to be counted among the proud members of the children of Avraham, Yitzchak, and Yaakov.

יום כיפור
Yom Kippur

_____ *Rabbi Dr. Abner Weiss*

*R*ABBON *Shimon ben Gamliel said: "There were no happier days for Israel than the 15th of Av and Yom Kippur"* (Taanis 4:8).

There are historical reasons for the joyful nature of the 15th of *Av*. Yom Kippur is associated with joy for an entirely different set of reasons. One of them is of special significance to today's *simcha*.

On its most profound level, Yom Kippur represents personal rebirth. This is experienced in a number of ways. Immersion in the *mikveh* on the eve of Yom Kippur is well nigh universally observed. Emergence from the living waters reminds us of our physical birth. After nine months in the amniotic fluid in the womb, we first experienced birth as our journey from a wet environment into a dry world. On the eve of Yom Kippur, we recreate this experience by our symbolic emergence from the womb of the *Shechinah,* reborn and revived. Significantly, it is the same act of emergence from the *mikveh* which transforms the convert into the newborn son or daughter of our father Avraham.

Our act of atonement on Yom Kippur has the same effect. Rambam points out that the truly penitent sinner is not the same person as he or she was *before* the act of repentance. *Teshuvah* and *kapparah* are thus also rebirth experiences.

We can understand the significance of the *Bris Milah* on a similarly profound level. It, too, is a birthing experience. Our emergence from our mothers' wombs is our *physical* birth. In this respect we are no different

_____
Rabbi Weiss is rav of Marble Arch Synagogue, London, England.

from other humans. Our entry into the covenant of Abraham is our *spiritual* birth. It introduces us into a life of religious commitment. It indicates our entrance into a system of values which both inform and transform us from the merely human into the spiritual human, or as Samson Raphael Hirsch puts it, "from *mensch* to *Yisrael mensch.*"

Physical and spiritual birth are vastly different. Once our physical birth is over it is over. Our entry into the convenant of Abraham, on the other hand, is an ongoing process. It involves both formal and informal education, and culminates when we reach religious maturity, accepting upon ourselves the yoke of the commandments. While the eight-day-old infant experiences *milah,* it is his parents who are challenged with the responsibility of his education and training.

Today's *simcha* celebrates the readiness of the parents to undertake this great challenge. Knowing them and their background as we do, leaves us with no doubt that their personal *simcha* will add immeasurably to the *simcha* of *Knesses Yisrael* — the entire Jewish people on this Yom Kippur.

Mazel tov, Mazel tov.

סוכות
Succos

Dr. David Luchins

AT FIRST BLUSH, THE HOLIDAY OF SUCCOS AND THE *MITZVAH* OF *BRIS MILAH* appear to have little in common. After all, Succos is the holiday that celebrates our oneness with *teva*, with nature. A *succah* whose *s'chach* has been altered by human hands from its natural state is not a kosher *succah*. The very essence of a *Bris* is to change *teva*, to improve upon the human body in a fashion that would not be *halachically* permissible if it were not an explicit *mitzvah*.

Succos is the holiday which celebrates our relationship with the nations of the world. In ancient times we offered *korbanos* on their behalf; today we offer our prayers in place of *korbanos*. And *Bris Milah*, since time immemorial, celebrates our uniqueness, our separateness from the nations of the world.

Thus, Succos and *Bris Milah* appear to represent unrelated, if not conflicting, themes. And yet, if we examine the Rabbinic literature, we discover an astonishing fact — the very festival of Succos has its *midrashic* roots in the very first *Bris Milah*.

Avraham, wracked with pain from his self-inflicted surgery, is being visited by Hashem when he spots three strangers at a distance. Excusing himself from the *Rebono Shel Olom*, Avraham rushes, in the heat of the desert sun, to plead with these travelers to turn aside and "rest under the shade of the tree and drink a bit of water" (*Bereishis* 18:4). And then he

Dr. Luchins is chairman of the Department of Political Science at Touro College and senior advisor to the Comptroller of the State of New York..

rushes to his herd to prepare calves for their pleasure.

And what is the Almighty's reaction to being "stood up" for three nomadic Arab wanderers? The Midrash reports that Hashem declared, "Because you offered them the shade of the tree, I will give your children the *mitzvah* of *succah*. Because you offered them a respite of water I will give your children the *mitzvah* of *nissuch hamayim* —water libations — on Succos. Because you offered them the flesh of a calf, I will give your children the *mitzvah* of offering 70 calves on behalf of the nations of the world during Succos."

Not only is this the earliest historical linkage between Succos and the nascent Jewish people but it may well be the only *midrashic* connection between this magnificent *chag* and Avraham *Avinu* — the first Jew.

What are *Chazal* telling us? What is it about the first *Bris Milah* that conjures up images of the Succos Festival?

Rabbi Shlomo Breuer, the sage of Frankfurt, suggests that the roots of this connection may well lie in another well-known Midrash.

When Avraham *Avinu* received the long awaited *mitzvah* of *Bris Milah*, he sought advice from his three closest friends and confidants, Aner, Eshkol, and Mamre.

The first two reacted in shock.

"You are an old man," one said, "you will be maiming yourself, if not causing your death."

"Your enemies have been waiting for such a moment," the second friend declared, "the relatives of the four kings you defeated will seek revenge on you as you recover helplessly from this serious surgery."

"Don't listen to them," Mamre declared, "the G-d that saved you from the fiery furnace and the four kings, who has guided and guarded your every step will surely protect you from any danger inherent in His command."

The first and obvious question is why Avraham — who leaped as a lad into a furnace without asking any questions and would as an old man rush to the *Akeidah* without consulting with anyone — this very Avraham would suddenly feel a need to consult with others before carrying out a Divine command?

Rav Breuer explains that Avraham was not consulting on whether to do the *mitzvah*. In his mind there could be no question or consultation on this account. Rather he was trying to gauge the best way to do this precious *mitzvah*. Should it be done privately or publicly? Since there was no Divine guidance on this point, Avraham had to find the most effective way to do the *mitzvah* while enhancing his mission to bring G-d's message to all humanity. Would news of this command frighten people off? Should it be done in private, particularly since it was not one of *the Sheva Mitzvos* of the *Bnei Noach* but would only be for Avraham's people? Why go public with a *mitzvah* that may lead to Avraham being seen as a freak, which will vitiate his message and lead to the death of his mission? Isn't this the moment his spiritual enemies had been waiting for?

Mamre inspired Avraham to go public, and, the Midrash tells us, Avraham then wrote letters to all the neighboring nations and tribes informing them of his decision in clear unambiguous terms.

But after the surgery the doubts as to the wisdom of this strategy begin to stir. It has been three long days since the *Bris* and not a single guest has come by to sample Sarah's and Avraham's renowned hospitality. Little did they realize that this lack of guests was an act of Divine kindness nurtured by an unnatural heat wave. On the contrary, Rav Breuer suggests, Avraham must have begun to think that Aner and Eshkol may have had a point. The word must be out that he is a self-mutilating lunatic. Small wonder that no one wants to visit with him anymore, much less stay overnight.

Hashem understands Avraham's anguish and sends three mysterious strangers to provide him with the longed for guests. Avraham is delighted. His *Bris Milah* may have made him different, but it has not shut him off from the rest of humanity. He rushes to embrace and entertain his guests. To assure them that they are all the children of the same creator, shaped in the image of the same G-d, touched by the same emotions, denizens, in a final sense, of the same world and citizens of the same race — the human race.

Hashem responds to Avraham's reaffirmation of his relationship with the rest of His creation by informing him of the *mitzvah* of *Chag HaSuccos* : the shade of the *succah* which, unimpeded by any manmade *chatziza*, declares our oneness with nature and nature's G-d; the water libations which celebrate the universal common denominator of life — the gift of water; and the *shivim korbanos* — our prayers and hopes for all humanity.

Avraham has demonstrated that *Bris Milah* may make us *different* but it may never make us *indifferent* to the rest of G-d's creatures and creations.

Our responsibilities to all of G-d's creatures permeate the *chag* of Succos — from the *korbanos* and נסוך המים to the very structure of the *succah*. Our oneness with humanity and nature is stressed in a fashion that enhances our uniqueness and mission.

Could there be a more appropriate time for this defining *mitzvah* of *Bris* than the holiday that owes its very allegorical origins to the events surrounding the very first *Bris Milah*?

May Hashem grant the רק הנמול the wisdom to always know how to cherish the message of both *Bris* and *succah* — of uniqueness and involvement, of celebrating *Am Yisrael's* mission both to its own people and to all of Hashem's creation.

הושענה רבה
Hoshanah Rabbah

_____ *Dr. Larry Ross*

*H*OSHANAH RABBAH, THE LAST DAY OF SUCCOS (6TH DAY IN ISRAEL, 7TH DAY IN the Diaspora), has a long history of being a special day. In the Mishnah (*Succah* 4:5-7), it is known as "the day of circling the Altar seven times;" R. Yehudah b. Beroka says it is known as "the day of beating the willow." The Mishnah also records the custom of the children who loosen their tied-together palm branches and eat their *esrogim*. Later, when the calendar was fixed and no longer dependent on the sighting of the new moon, it was stipulated that Rosh Hashanah could not fall on Sunday so that *Hoshanah Rabbah* would not come out on Shabbos, because that would interfere with many of its observances. At least for the last seven hundred years, *Hoshanah Rabbah* has been regarded as *Yom Kippur Katan* (the little Yom Kippur), the day on which one's verdict is sealed or delivered, perhaps because on the holiday of Succos, the world is judged for rain (*Mishnah Rosh Hashanah* 1:2). For this reason the *chazzan* customarily dons a *kittel*.

Because of its uniqueness, *Hoshanah Rabbah* has many distinguishing customs. Many people learn Torah part or all of the night, especially *Sefer Devarim* and *Sefer Tehillim,* the latter composed by King David who is the Guest ("*Ushpiz*") of the last night of Succos. The Midrash records the story of King David who once felt sad to be naked until he realized that he had a sign of the Covenant, i.e., a *Bris*, on his body. One interpretation of this

_____
Dr. Ross is Assistant Professor of Medicine at the Albert Einstein College of Medicine, Bronx, New York and a member of the Community Synagogue of Monsey, New York.

Midrash is that we are all "clothed in our *Mitzvos.*" However, when carefully examined, a person's *Mitzvos* may well turn out to be imperfectly performed or tinged with ulterior motives. Not so *Bris Milah,* and certainly not from the perspective of the child being circumcised. He has truly done his part wholeheartedly, בלב שלם. Perhaps this is the explanation for our saying at a *Bris,* "Just as he has entered into the Covenant, so may he enter the Torah, the marriage canopy, and good deeds."

King David, we are told, was awakened by the north wind blowing through his harp at midnight, and would arise and spend the rest of the night singing praises to G-d. We, therefore, recite the praises (*Tehillim*) composed by King David as part of the *Tikkun* (Purification), of the night of *Hoshanah Rabbah.*

This morning's service was marked by several unique features. The introductory psalms (*Pesukai D'zimrah*) we recited were those of Shabbos or *Yom Tov,* though there is no prohibition of work on *Hoshanah Rabbah.* As on all the days of Succos, the Torah was read. The father of the רך הנמול was one of the four people called to the Torah. Indeed, he and a bridegroom during the first week of marriage are especially designated to be called to the Torah, perhaps for the same reason: there can be no Torah without Jews to support it, and the *mitzvah* of "Be fruitful and multiply" (פרו ורבו) depends on Jewish marriage and of course on *Bris Milah.*

Just as today's *Bris* was performed wholeheartedly on this special and unique *Yom Tov,* so may the parents merit to raise their son בלב שלם to a life of Torah and *Mitzvos.* Mazel Tov!

שמיני עצרת
Shemini Atzeres

_____ *Rabbi Avromy Fein*

AS WE USHER OUT THE JEWISH HOLIDAY SEASON BY CELEBRATING THE *YOM Tov* of Shemini Atzeres in conjunction with a *Bris Milah,* one contemplates the significance of the "eighth" day in Judaism. Rashi, in *Vayikra* 23:36, teaches us that the Almighty finds it difficult to separate from His children after so many days of *Yomin Tovim.* To facilitate this separation, Hashem added the additional *Yom Tov* of Shemini Atzeres.

The Sochotchover Rebbe, more popularly known as the *Shem M'Shmuel,* asks how this additional day of *Yom Tov* will alleviate the difficulty of our leaving. It would seem that the added day would only augment the difficulty. The *Shem M'Shmuel* suggests the following answer: The number seven represents a natural status, as we find with the six days of Creation and the seventh day of rest. The seven days of the week symbolize man's very existence, combining both the spiritual (Shabbos) along with the physical (weekdays). However, "eight" represents a status beyond nature, perhaps even a mystical level. "Eight" symbolizes man's ability to transcend the limitations of physical existence. For example, the *Talmud Bavli, Arachin* 13b states that the harp used in the Temple had seven strings, while in Messianic times, the harp will have eight strings. Our seven days of Succos allow us to reinvigorate our relationship with Hashem and draw closer to Him. But what assurance is there that the precious bond forged on Succos will endure throughout the following year? Hashem, therefore, granted us the holiday of Shemini Atzeres as a

_____
Rabbi Fein is a practicing attorney in Suffern, New York and is a weekly lecturer at the Riverdale Jewish Center.

guarantor. This eighth day will elevate us beyond the realm of nature, and will ensure that this bond will remain beyond the holiday itself.

Onkeles translates the word *atzeres* to mean *kenishin* (ingathering). Shemini Atzeres celebrates the ingathering and unity of the Jewish people. It is interesting to note that another name for the festival of Succos is *Chag HaAsif* — the holiday of ingathering! Reb Yehuda Arye Leib Alter of Ger, also known as the *Sfas Emes,* explains that the effect of this unity experienced by the Jewish people during Succos will remain beyond the festival itself through our observance of Shemini Atzeres — the magical eighth day. The Torah, in describing Shemini Atzeres says, ". . . on the eighth day an *atzeres* (assembly) will be for you" (*Bamidbar* 29:35). Shemini Atzeres allows us to take the unity attained during Succos and make it part of our lives throughout the year.

Similarly, the *Bris Milah* is performed on the eighth day of the newborn boy's life. The young baby will encounter many challenges throughout his life. We pray that a close bond with Hashem will be everlasting and enable him to withstand the difficult challenges ahead. We know that nothing is random in Judaism. The eighth day was chosen by Hashem for the performance of the *Bris Milah* to instill in the newborn baby the potential to ascend beyond nature and achieve great heights. How much more so is this the case when the eighth day of a baby's life coincides with Shemini Atzeres, the eighth day of celebrating the unique relationship between *Am Yisrael* and Hashem!

It is notable that, according to the *Sfas Emes,* both the holidays of Shemini Atzeres and Shavuos are called *Atzeres* (*Pesachim* 68b). These two holidays revolve around the theme of Torah. Shavuos celebrates the *receiving* (and therefore, the beginning) of Torah, and Shemini Atzeres celebrates the *completion* of the Torah. Shavuos is the time of year that the *Bikurim* (new fruit) are brought to Jerusalem. Our Sages teach us that Shavuos is actually the period of judgment for the fruit trees, as we bring forth nature's produce to give thanks for its bounty. Shemini Atzeres is the time of year we pray for rain. We pray for the nourishment that will feed the earth and give it the potential to allow its trees and plants to grow and flourish. On Shemini Atzeres we pray for the potential, whereas on Shavuos, we have the actual product in hand.

For the רך הנמול whose *Bris Milah* coincides with the holiday of Shemini Atzeres, we also pray for his potential — to grow and flourish as a *ben Torah* and a source of pride to his family and *Am Yisrael.*

שמחת תורה
Simchas Torah

_____ *Rabbi Daniel M. Hartstein*

תורה צוה לנו משה מורשה קהלת יעקב — "THE TORAH THAT MOSES COMMANDED us is the heritage of the Congregation of Jacob" (*Devarim* 33:4).

The last *Parshah* in the Torah gives us insight into the essence of the entire Torah. תורה צוה לנו משה is the first *pasuk* a Jew says upon rising in the morning, and it is one of the first *pesukim* we teach our children. It is of utmost importance that at the celebration and completion of the Torah we understand the Torah's message in this *pasuk*.

Traditionally the word "*Morasha*" is interpreted as an inheritance, a legacy. This implies that the Torah was bequeathed to the nation of Israel as an inheritance. It is incumbent upon each father to transmit the Torah to his son, as it was received thousands of years ago from Moshe.

Rabbi Yehoshua Leib Diskin explained that the word *Morasha* is not simply an inheritance. An inheritor can do whatever he pleases with the inheritance he has received. There is no judge and jury who can question his motives and actions. However, a *Morasha* is drastically different. This form of inheritance must be safeguarded for his entire life, so that one day he will be able to pass it on to his children and so on through the generations.

It is with this insight that we can shed light on the Talmud *Pesachim* (49b) stating — "Do not read it מורשה — inheritance, read it מאורשה — betrothed." Our Sages add this explanation to clarify that the Torah may

_____

Rabbi Hartstein is currently a director at Net2Phone and is a member of the Beit Midrash of Bergen County.

not be dismissed as a mere "inheritance." The term "betrothed" refers to marriage. This is the unique relationship we have with Hashem and His Torah. We must preserve and transmit the Torah with the same love and affection a new groom shows for his bride. It is with this type of fervor that the Torah is eternalized, as if we were standing at Sinai. A child must understand that *everyday* is "Simchas Torah" in our eyes. Although, we do not physically dance with the Torah on a daily basis, we must convey to our children that *spiritually,* in our hearts and souls, we are constantly dancing with the love of Torah.

On the auspicious day of bringing a son into the Jewish nation, at his *Bris Milah,* through the covenant of our forefather Abraham, one must recognize the proper path in which the Torah must be transmitted to his son — as a true heritage rather than a mere inheritance.

It is interesting to note that the Torah uses the word *Morasha* in only one other place: *"I shall bring you to the land about which I raised My hand to give it to Abraham, Isaac, and Jacob and I shall give it to you as a heritage (מורשה) — I am Hashem" (Shemos 6:8).*

Based on our understanding of *Morasha* we can appreciate the true meaning of inheriting the Land of Israel. The *Baal HaTurim* notes that in the merit of those who transmit the Torah from generation to generation, as a *Morasha,* the Nation of Israel will be granted the *zechus* to truly inherit the land of Israel. May we be fortunate to see this speedily in our day.

Our hope and prayer is that the parents should be *zocheh* to transmit the מורשה of Torah to their new son, and raise him to a life of Torah and *maasim tovim.*

חנוכה
Chanukah

_____ *Rabbi Yisroel Epstein*

THE FIRST THOUGHT THAT COMES TO MIND WHEN CELEBRATING THE OCCASION of a *bris* on Chanukah is the commonality of eight days: eight days of Chanukah; eight days from birth to *bris*. But is this parallel just a coincidence or does a deeper significance lie beneath its surface?

In Jewish law and lore, the number seven represents a complete cycle in the physical realm. The seven days of the week stem from seven days of Creation. The agricultural cycle of years is seven, culminating with *Shemittah*. And the world, we are told in *Kabbalah*, evolves with seven millennia in mind.

Eight, however, signifies the next stage, going beyond the physical to the metaphysical realm. On Chanukah, this spirituality is manifested in the lights we kindle each night. In a traditional sense, the eight days celebrate the miracle of the lights of the *menorah*, which burned long beyond their physical properties ought to have allowed. These lights transcended nature; they became supernatural lights.

In contemporary times, this supernatural trend continues. Lighting the Chanukah *menorah* is, somewhat surprisingly, the most popular of all holiday activities among Jews. A recent survey by the Jewish Federation found that 93 percent of Jews light Chanukah candles, more than attend a Pesach Seder or fast on Yom Kippur!

Almost all Jews have a special attachment to Chanukah. What accounts for it? What is so unique about these lights that they continue to burn

_____

Rabbi Epstein is associate editor of Torah Insights *published by the Orthodox Union.*

almost two thousand years after the destruction of the Holy Temple?

Bris Milah — the covenant of Abraham that binds every Jew to God and His Torah — was outlawed by the Hellenists. Such mutilation, in their eyes, had no place in a society that worshipped the human figure. Man's body was his temple.

The Torah mocks such base beliefs. There is no higher purpose to be found in the physical realm as an end in itself. The body is uplifted only when spirituality — translated as the Will of God, as told to us in the Torah — is infused into its physical form. Man's mundane existence is elevated by his embrace of the spiritual and his commitment to imprint it on his physicality.

Bris Milah accomplishes just that. Man takes his most private limb, a tool used for potentially the most holy and potentially the most profane act, and marks it for God. In this way, *milah* elevates the body, turning it from an independent figure into a vehicle for completeness in the service of God.

The irony is that what the Greeks considered an act of mutilation is, in fact, an act of completion. The Midrash states that man is only complete when he is circumcised.

Rav Shimon Schwab, *zt"l*, points out that the word *milah* means to mix. The *bris* is called *milah* "because with the removal of the foreskin, the sanctity of Israel spreads through the corporeal body." In this manner, he writes, man is combined into a "man of spirit" and a "man of action."

This act infuriated the Hellenists, whose games were played in the nude in order to flaunt the human form. So threatened were they by the notion of *milah* that they targeted it specifically and made its practice punishable by death. The *Chashmona'im* responded, and defended not simply this *mitzvah*, but the worldview that it represented: Our bodies are not ours but God's; they are not to be devoted to physical gain but to spiritual pursuit.

In *Beis Yosef*, Rav Yosef Karo, codifier of Jewish law, asks his famous Chanukah question: If the *Chashmona'im* found enough oil to burn for one day, then the miracle of the oil was only for the following seven days. Why do we not celebrate Chanukah for seven days instead of eight?

The *Beis Yosef* gives several answers, as do many other commentaries. One commentary, the *Pri Chadash*, answers that the first day is to celebrate the miracle of the *Chashmona'im*'s victory over the Greeks.

That victory is cited in our prayers, which describes how God "delivered the strong into the hands of the weak, the many into the hands of the few, the defiled into the hands of the pure." Our military victory was not one of strategic genius, but of Divine intervention, brought about by our defense of Torah and *Mitzvos* in the face of a dangerous world, by our willingness to wage war for, among other *mitzvos,* the *mitzvah* of *Bris Milah.* The *Chashmona'im* stood up to a Hellenist society that promoted values diametrically opposed to our Torah, and by doing so merited the resumption of the Temple service, including the lighting of the *menorah.*

The miracle of Chanukah is its perseverance throughout the generations, its small candles casting long rays of light down the dark corridor of a long and frightening exile. Despite all obstacles, despite persecution and hatred, the Jewish people remain. We survive. We flourish.

Our newest Jew lies before us filled with this new potential, the potential to be a Jew of unique greatness, to enter, as we bless him, "the realm of Torah, marriage, and good deeds." Torah study will be his basis for knowledge and wisdom, for guidance and inspiration. Marriage will sanctify his body and soul, perpetuating a family lifestyle that contributes to the strength and longevity of the Jewish people. And good deeds will be the result of his study and family values — charity, compassion, and contribution to the community.

Chanukah means dedication. Today, his parents dedicate themselves to raise this infant as a Torah Jew in a home suffused with Torah values. We are, therefore, confident that "גדול יהיה,, — he will grow up to mature not just physically, but spiritually; to graduate to greater and greater heights of accomplishment in Torah and *Mitzvos;* to love and honor God; to be a source of pride to our great nation, Israel; and to be a source of light in a sea of darkness, illuminating the way for generations of Jews to return to their heritage, the Divine directive that is our lot and our legacy.

פורים
Purim

Rabbi Doniel Z. Kramer

ONE OF THE MOST FAMOUS PHRASES IN *MEGILLAS ESTHER* IS NOT ONLY ONE OF the four verses which is recited by the congregation as well as the reader during the *Megillah* reading, but is also recited in the *Havdalah* service which concludes the Shabbos. In fact, it is the only phrase in the *Havdalah* that the assemblage utters aloud. This verse is, ליהודים היתה אורה ושמחה וששון ויקר — "The Jews had Light, and Gladness, Joy, and Honor" (8:16).

In the tractate *Megillah,* 16b, Rabbi Yehudah teaches: אורה — *Light,* refers to Torah; שמחה — *Gladness,* refers to *Yom Tov* (the festivals); ששון — *Joy,* refers to the rite of circumcision; and יקר — *Honor,* refers to *Tefillin.* The proof-text for the assumption that ששון refers to circumcision is based upon verse 162 in *Tehillim,* Chapter 119, which begins with a similar kind of word — שש. The verse is, שש אנכי על אמרתך כמוצא שלל רב — "I rejoice at Your word, as one who finds great booty." *Rashi* explains that "Your word" (אמרתך) refers to the fact that God gave the *mitzvah* of circumcision to our Patriarch Abraham, utilizing a similar Hebrew word, ויאמר, as opposed to the stronger word for speaking, וידבר.

This explanation is a somewhat tenuous one, for other commandments also are introduced with the word, ויאמר. In addition, there is no particular joy involved for the individual being circumcised during the actual act of *Bris Milah. Rashi* explains that the joy referred to is expressive of what King David realized when he was in the bath house, stripped of all external

Rabbi Kramer is Director of the United Jewish Communities Rabbinic Cabinet, New York City.

appurtenances of *mitzvos*, such as *Tzitzis* and *Tefillin*. A sense of joy overcame him when he realized that even in that naked setting, he still bore the sign of the Covenant of Circumcision. The fact that this *mitzvah* was indelibly impressed upon him delighted him greatly.

The *Torah Temimah* explains that perhaps the real proof of the fact that ששון refers to *Milah* comes from the latter part of the proof-text, כמוצא שלל רב, "...as one who finds great booty." He maintains that the *mitzvah* of circumcision is really an effortless one for the male who bears its sign. He does not have to do any action *directly*, and the act itself takes but a few seconds. The pain of circumcision passes very quickly, but the *mitzvah* remains with him forever. The *Torah Temimah* compares this to finding a great treasure for which one did not have to expend much effort, but whose riches and rewards one enjoys far into the future. The reward of *Bris Milah* truly is for a lifetime.

We can now understand why, after the Purim victory, the Jews especially celebrated the fact that they had "light and gladness and joy and honor." No longer threatened with either physical or spiritual annihilation, they could once again study Torah, much like the Torah verses that were learned by the young children who gave Mordechai the moral fortitude to fight the evil edict of Haman. Purim did become a *Yom Tov*, a day of gladness, and יקר, *Tefillin*, particularly the *Tefillin* on the head which mark the fact that Jews could once again proudly hold up their heads and bear the symbol of God with pride and in prayer. ששון, joy, marking the *mitzvah* of circumcision upon their very bodies, was of particular importance, as they realized that they had been facing the threat of physical death, and Purim represented renewed life. Precisely when their physical existence was so threatened, the Jews especially enjoyed the opportunity to mark the *mitzvah* that represented a *physical* commitment to God's word.

Therefore, it is most meaningful when a baby is blessed with the opportunity to have his *Bris* on Purim day. This confirms the fact that on this day we celebrate our resurrection as a people and remind ourselves of our commitment to serve God, both physically as well as metaphysically.

What is unique about a *Bris* on Purim day is that it also means in most cases, that the baby was born eight days beforehand, on the seventh day of Adar, which is both the birthday and *yahrtzeit* of Moshe *Rabbeinu*.

Moshe lived for 120 complete years (the day of his death was also on the day of his birth), and he merited that his life should end with a kiss of death from the Almighty. There was no physical pain or bodily deterioration, and his sight was not diminished nor did his strength ebb. As Moshe died a perfect man, so was he born, for we are taught that he was born already circumcised and complete. Therefore, one who was born on the day of Moshe's birthday and on Purim becomes complete with a *Bris Milah* especially merits the gifts of this verse from *Megillas Esther*. As Moshe gave us the Torah, on Purim the Jews marked the fact that light was restored to them through the gift of Torah, and we know that likewise this will be a gift for the new-born baby who has been circumcised this day. Normally, the occasion of a *Bris Milah* is a private festival for the immediate family; however, today, the entire people of Israel celebrate this festivity. Unlike the other festivals, on Purim day, *Tefillin* are worn for they remind us of the fact that it was Moshe himself who perceived the Almighty's *Tefillin* when God instructed him in the recitation of the Thirteen Attributes of Divine Mercy. Customarily, *Tefillin* are worn by those involved in the circumcision ceremony, and we particularly pray that as this baby, in thirteen years time, will put on his own *Tefillin,* may he truly merit also to partake of the glory of God's *Tefillin.*

At the conclusion of Shabbos, as we prepare for another work week, we recite this verse from *Esther,* "The Jews had Light and Gladness and Joy and Honor ," and add the phrase, כן תהיה לנו — "And so may it be with us." When we can take a mundane work week and infuse it with the spirit of the outgoing Shabbos so that the sense of holiness and sacredness can permeate the entire week, that is not only the hope of *Motzaei Shabbos,* but also the gift of the Jews of Shushan. The observance of Purim gave them strength to make all of their future days significant.

May it be God's will that all of the hopes and prayers of Purim day that were fulfilled for the Jews of Shushan be the lot of the רך הנמול too. The Torah sums up the life of Moshe and calls him, "*Eved Hashem*" — Servant of God. Like Moshe, may this baby mature to be an "*Eved Hashem*"; and like Mordechai, the Jew, as the final verse of the *Megillah* concludes, may he be "Great among the Jews and accepted by the multitude of his brethren, seeking the good welfare of his people, and speaking peace to all his seed." Amen.

שבת הגדול
Shabbos HaGadol

Rabbi Jay Braverman

WE ARE PRIVILEGED TO CELEBRATE A _BRIS_ THIS MORNING, AT A VERY auspicious time— on the Shabbos before Pesach, known as _Shabbos HaGadol_. One explanation given as to why it is called "_Shabbos HaGadol_" is in reference to the next-to-last verse of the _Haftarah_, taken from the prophet Malachi: הנה אנכי שולח לכם את אליהו הנביא לפני בוא יום ה' הגדול והנורא — "Behold — I send you Elijah the Prophet, before the great and awesome day of Hashem" (3:23).

This _Haftarah_ is from the very last chapter in the Prophets. We are urged to remember the teachings of Moshe, in order to be constantly prepared for the arrival of the prophet Eliyahu, who will herald the coming of the _Moshiach,_ and the Day of Judgment.

Eliyahu the Prophet is the guest of honor at every _Bris;_ we even reserve a chair for him, כסא של אליהו. Rabbi Moshe Glustein, the Dean and Rosh Yeshiva at the Yeshiva Gedola in Montreal, explained why, specifically, Eliyahu was given this great honor to be the representative of Hashem at every _Bris_. This can be traced back to the origin of the _Bris_ between Hashem and Avraham (_Bereishis_ 17:4-14). A _Bris_ is a convenant or agreement, which requires the presence of _two_ parties, and the obligations of both must clearly be defined. Hashem's obligation (vs. 4-8) includes the multiplying of Avraham's offspring, being the Jewish People's G-d forever, and giving them the entire land of Canaan as an everlasting possession.

Rabbi Braverman is a retired educator who has been involved in Jewish education his entire professional life.

The obligation of Avraham and his descendants (vs. 9-14) includes faithfully upholding this covenant (the moral and spiritual aspects; see the comment of Rabbi Samson Raphael Hirsch), as well as the *sign* of the covenant— the circumcision of every male on the eighth day. The prophet Eliyahu, who ascended to heaven in a chariot of fire, represents G-d, the second "party," at each *Bris.* (See the commentary of *Sforno* to *Bereishis* 12:1, the first verse in *Vayeira.*)

With this in mind, the traditional prayer recited several times at every *Bris,* takes on an added dimension: כשם שנכנס לברית כן יכנס לתורה ולחפה ולמעשים טובים — "Just as he (Eliyahu, the representative of G-d) has accompanied the infant as he entered the Covenant (of Abraham), so may Eliyahu accompany him throughout life as he studies Torah, enters under the marriage canopy and performs good deeds."

The last verse in the *Haftarah* from Malachi describes the final mission of Eliyahu before the Judgment Day, at the time of *Moshiach*: והשיב לב אבות על בנים, ולב בנים על אבותם — "He shall restore the heart of the fathers to the children, and the heart of children to their fathers" (3:24). Eliyahu will bridge, heal, and make peace between generations in the future, just as he served as a bridge between heaven and earth, in the past. Since he is present at every *Bris,* it is appropriate for **him** to unite the generations together before the coming of the *Moshiach.* He is, thus, the precursor of the ultimate redemption. Therefore, a special cup of wine, כוס אליהו, in his honor, graces, every *Seder* Table.

May the Prophet Eliyahu, present at our *Bris* today, accompany the child through all the important stages of his life, and may he come speedily, in our days, to usher in the Messianic Era. Amen.

פסח

Pesach

_____ *Rabbi Joseph A. Grunblatt*

THE HOLIDAY "PESACH," AS IT IS CALLED IN HALACHIC LITERATURE (IN THE Torah the word *Pesach* refers to the *Korban Pesach*), derives its name from the *Korban Pesach*, the Paschal lamb consumed at the *Seder* when we had our *Beis Hamikdash*. The two *mitzvos* — *Pesach* and *Bris Milah* have a somewhat symbiotic relationship. First of all they are the only two *Mitzvos Asseh* (positive commandments) whose deliberate omission evokes "*Kores*," a heavenly penalty of premature death.

One may not sacrifice, nor partake, in the eating of the *Korban Pesach* if one is uncircumcised. Furthermore, one cannot participate in *Pesach* if one's minor male children were not circumcised [The importance of *Milah* as a prerequisite can be found in *Shemos* 12:43-49 and a number of Rabbinic texts, specifically Talmud *Bavli Pesachim* 96a.]

Looking at it a little more deeply one can recognize the similarities of the existential experience of Avraham *Avinu*, the first individual Jew (if not in the *halachic* sense but certainly in the historical sense), and the Jewish people as a nation when they sacrificed the *Korban Pesach* and prepared to leave Egypt. Sociologically and culturally Avraham left his "natural habitat" — ... לך לך מארצך. He had to leave the land and home in which he was born and raised to seek the "promised land." He had to break the idols of his environment and to some extent he became alienated from the society of his day.

_____

Rabbi Grunblatt is rav of the Queens Jewish Center & Talmud Torah, Forest Hills, New York.

When the Jews left Egypt they left the country where they were born and raised (for several generations). They had, according to Rabbinic tradition, become quite acculturated in Egypt. The Rabbis tell us that at first they filled the theaters and sports arenas of Egypt. Indeed, subsequent to enslavement they seemed to have adopted the idols of Egypt and even discontinued the tradition of circumcision. Our Sages comment on the verse: "draw and take unto yourself a lamb (the Paschal lamb. . .)" — "draw away from *Avodah Zarah*" (idolatry).

Avraham *Avinu's* covenant was sealed with *Bris Milah*. In the *berachah* of *Bris Milah* are the words "and sealed his offspring with the sign of the holy covenant." The Exodus began with the *Seder* night and concluded with the giving of the Torah seven weeks later which was the *"chasimah,"* the seal of our national existence. Neither our *Bris Milah* nor our national *Bris* as an *Am HaTorah* can be rescinded. It can only be violated.

There were very similar byproducts of the *chasimah* of Avraham as an individual and *Am Yisrael* as a nation. Midrash tells us at the end of *"Lech Lecha"* when Avraham was given the *mitzvah* of *Milah,* he worried about his relationship with the world at large: "Until now so many people would come and see me, but now (that I am distinctly different) people will no longer come and associate with me." Hashem's reply was, "But now I will visit you;" this is why we read in *Vayeira* — "and Hashem appeared to Abraham." There was a trade-off — a level of alienation from the rest of the world but a more intense relationship with Hashem. The Exodus was more than "taking one nation from amidst a nation" (*Devarim* 4:34), it was also from amidst *all* the nations. In the words of Bilaam who hated the Jews most but knew them best: "This is a nation that dwells alone and is not counted amongst the nations" (*Bamidbar* 23:9). As much as we care for and participate in the welfare of all mankind there is and always will be a level of alienation because of our special status, role, and *"Ol Mitzvos",* the "Jewish Man's Burden."

The historical evolvement of the Jewish people is reenacted when a Jewish child is added to *Klal Yisrael.* He first enters the Abramic experience by receiving the seal of the covenant as an individual. That may explain the somewhat strange second *berachah* recited at the *Bris* — "who commanded us to bring him into the covenant of Abraham." It is well-known that the Rambam insists that the *Mitzvos* given before Sinai are observed now because they were given at Sinai and not because of their proper observance. What the *berachah* is saying is that by performing *Bris Milah* (as commanded at Sinai) we reenact the experience of Avraham *Avinu*. His differentiation now begins and to some extent his alienation too. The child will soon learn that he cannot do many things that most other children in the world can do, and that he is expected to do things that are strange and alien to most children in the world. He has to be taught and inspired that he will be somewhat less involved in the world at large but more intimate with Hashem. "As he entered the *Bris* so may he enter to Torah, marriage and good deeds" — As he matures, becomes socialized, and responsible, he relives the covenant of the Exodus and Sinai by assuming full Torah responsibility of *Mitzvos*, family and community involvement as a full-fledged member of *Klal Yisrael.*

Avraham was a pioneer and had no parents to help him. In fact, they were a hindrance to practicing his discovered truth. The Jews in Egypt did have the tribe of Levi, which seemed to have maintained tradition. Yet, the overall impact was not great. Fortunate are the children born to parents that care, and into communities that provide the ambiance for the constant renewal of the covenant.

שבועות

Shavuos

_____ *Rabbi Tzvi Flaum*

THE *NETZIV* POINTS OUT, IN HIS ANALYSIS OF *SEFER BEREISHIS*, THAT WHEN Avraham was commanded to perform the *mitzvah* of *Bris Milah* his name was changed from Avram to Avraham. The Torah explains that this name change signified that up until now he was the spiritual father of Aram. Henceforth, he would be the spiritual father of the entire world, as the Torah says: כי אב המון גוים נתתיך — "for I have made you the father of a multitude of nations" (*Bereishis* 17:5).

The *Netziv* emphasizes that at this juncture of Avraham's spiritual and communal life, he was given a two-fold mission. The first part of the mission was to spiritually intensify both *his* essence and that of his nuclear family through the performance of *Bris Milah*, as the Torah says: התהלך לפני והיה תמים — "Walk before Me [by performing the circumcision] and become spiritually perfect" (ibid. 17:1).

The *mitzvah* of circumcision was going to intensify his duty of דביקות, devotion to הקב"ה and catapult him onto a unique spiritual plane. The second part of his mission was to reach out to mankind and spiritually uplift them by bringing them to a belief of pure monotheism, and making sure that they adhere to their Noahide laws. To summarize, we see that Avraham's mission involved, on the one hand, a particularist's endeavor of self-perfection, and, on the other hand, a universalist's responsibility of bringing the entire world closer to Hashem.

The *Netziv* continues and explains that this mission of Avraham's was

_____

Rabbi Flaum is rav of Congregation Kneseth Israel, Far Rockaway, New York.

repeated to *Klal Yisrael* as they stood at the foot of Har Sinai.

Hashem said to them: ואתם תהיו לי ממלכת כהנים וגוי קדוש — "You shall be to Me a Nation of Priests and a Holy Nation" (*Shemos* 19:6).

Klal Yisrael, the successors of Avraham *Avinu*, were, likewise, given a two-fold mission. The first part of their mission was to become a גוי קדוש, a holy nation through the *Bris Milah* — immersing in a *mikvah,* and accepting תרי"ג מצות through נעשה ונשמע. This, in turn, defined their aspiration as particularists. The second part of their mission was to become a ממלכת כהנים, a Nation of Priests, which is interpreted to mean that they were going to serve as an אור לגויים, a spiritual light and guide to the nations of the world and bring them back to the pure Noahide monotheistic worship of G-d. This universalistic mission would bring the world closer to its final spiritual fulfillment, as Hashem had forecast in the words of the Torah: ביום ההוא יהיה ה' אחד ושמו אחד — "That day Hashem and His Name will be One" (*Zechariah* 14:9).

In contemporary times, we are very involved with our mandate of being a גוי קדוש, and therefore we are very conscientious about observing all the minutiae of *Halachah* as well as studying the holy Torah. However, the *Netziv* teaches us in the aforementioned thesis, that we have, likewise, a universal mission that must be adhered to. We must realize our responsibility to serve as spiritual, ethical and moral role models for the world at large. By fulfilling our mandate as Hashem's Chosen Nation, we will, hopefully, bring the world back to a pure monotheistic belief in Hashem, which will serve as the conduit for the fulfillment of the Messianic dream, as it is described and elaborated upon by our Holy Prophets.

On this *Yom Tov* of *Matan Torah* when we are celebrating the joyous occasion of a *Bris Milah* we want to give the parents and the רך הנמול the following *berachah*: May you be *zocheh* to raise your newborn son to fulfill his two-fold mission. Not only should be he able to uplift *himself* spiritually through Torah and *maasim tovim;* but may he also accept the broader mission of conveying Hashem's message to the world which emanates from within.

Insightful Essays

Attendance at a Bris Milah: Spectator or Participant?

_____ *Rabbi J. Simcha Cohen*

Question: IS SOMEONE WHO ATTENDS A *BRIS MILAH* MERELY A SPECTATOR OR considered as one involved in the actual performance of a *Mitzvah*?

Response: It is known that the *Kohen Gadol* performed several functions on Yom Kippur. He read from the Torah and also brought a number of sacrifices. The Mishnah reports that "He who sees the high priest when he reads (the Torah) does not see the (sacrifices of) the bullock and he-goat that were being burnt . . . (Why?). Not that he (the observer) was not permitted to do so, but because the distance between both activities was great and both rites were performed at the same time (*Yoma* 68b). Commenting upon this Mishnah, the Gemara was concerned with the necessity to detail that it was permissible (should it have been possible) for a person to observe *both* the ritual of the burning of the *korban* (sacrifice) as well as the *Kohen Gadol's* reading of the Torah. Was it not self-evident that both acts were permissible for observers to watch as well as to go from one to another? To this the Talmud notes that there is a Talmudic precept that might appear to be violated. It is the rule that one does not leave one *mitzvah* to attend to another. The Talmud questions, "and what *mitzvah* is here?" namely, spectators are not performing any *mitzvah*. To this the Talmud responds that there is the *mitzvah* of "in the multitude of the people there is the king's glory," ברוב עם. Rashi notes

_____

Rabbi Cohen is rav of the Mizrachi Kehilla in Melbourne, Australia.

that, generally, it is prohibited to leave one *mitzvah* to perform another. The reason why it is permitted to leave the observation of either of these *mitzvos* is that the *spectators* were not actually involved in the *performance* of the *mitzvah* itself (*Yoma* 70a).

Indeed, this indicates that had the people observing the *Kohen Gadol* been actual *participants* in the *mitzvah,* then they would *not* have been permitted to leave. Accordingly, a spectator observing the performance of a *mitzvah* need not remain till the *mitzvah* is concluded. Yet this is not the case when one actually performs a *mitzvah*. When a person actually performs a *mitzvah* there is a general rule that "whoever commences a *mitzvah* should conclude it" (המתחיל במצוה אומרים לו גמר).

Of interest is the following conception of the *B'nai Yissaschar* concerning the function of those who merely attend a *Bris Milah*. Citing a midrash as the source, he contends that G-d decreed that Eliyahu, the prophet, should be in attendance at every *Bris Milah*. To this Eliyahu demurred, saying that it is known that his character is such that he cannot tolerate sinners. Accordingly, should the father of the child be a sinner, Eliyahu would not be able to tolerate such sin (the implication was that Eliyahu might attack the father of the child for being sinful). To this the Almighty responded that He would forgive the sins of a father who has his child circumcised. Eliyahu further was perturbed about the status of religious observance of those who merely attended the *Bris Milah*. Perhaps, suggested Eliyahu, there would be among the participants Jews who sinned and would therefore incur the prophet's anger (again implying Eliyahu's presence might cause more harm than good). To this question G-d responded that He would forgive the sins of all who observed the performance of the circumcision. Another midrash is quoted that maintains that whoever stands and observes the child placed on the chair of Eliyahu (כסא של אליהו) is forgiven for all sin (*B'nai Yissaschar, Maamarai Tishrei Maamar* 4, *Derush* 7).

This midrash strongly suggests that a witness to a circumcision is not merely a spectator to a *mitzvah*. No, a *Bris Milah* has the unique power to transform the sins of *all* those present. All guests in attendance are involved with the *mitzvah* of *teshuvah* (repentance). Who would leave such a scene? Indeed, all would no doubt be obligated to remain until the *mitzvah* was concluded so as to be graced with the special powers of atonement.

Bris Milah —
A Non-Contingent Mitzvah

_____ *Rabbi Zalman I. Posner*

T HE FIRST TO HAVE A *BRIS MILAH* AFTER AVRAHAM HIMSELF WAS HIS SON, Yishmael, a thirteen-year-old boy. Yitchak was born a year later and had his *Bris* at eight days. Yishmael would taunt Yitzchak, "You didn't know what was happening at your *Bris,* but I willingly accepted mine, because I understood and believed. That makes my *Bris* superior to yours." Sounds reasonable. Why, indeed, shouldn't the *Bris* be held at the age of reason, *a la Yishmael?*

The human intelligence is in a constant state of flux, changing all the time. What was an absolute fact yesterday is shown today to be in error. For example, for countless centuries it was a "fact" that the sun revolves around the earth. Then Copernicus demonstrated that the earth circles the sun — possibly the greatest blow to the believers of that time. Then this absolute "fact" is undermined by Einstein, so that either view is acceptable. Tomorrow? Who knows?

Faith predicated on science, on reason, on the evidence of our eyes and experience, is tentative at best. As science shifts faith changes, or is simply abandoned as obsolete and irrelevant.

The Jews' commitment to Hashem and Torah and *Mitzvos* must not be contingent — not on his understanding, not on society's norms, not because a duly grateful G-d rewards him with all kinds of blessings.

Yishmael accepted the *Bris* because it passed his tests of rationality. When he learned later that he would not be Avraham's heir, off he went,

_____

Rabbi Posner is rav of Congregation Sherith Israel, Nashville,Tennessee.

and still later he returned, acknowledging that Yitzchak and his faith were superior.

Yitzchak had to go on the altar for his faith — and he went. His children endured destruction, exile, persecution, crusades, pogroms, until that last and greatest horror — the Holocaust. But Yitzchak and his children remained committed to that *Bris*. Their commitment was not contingent, because they enter the *Bris* at eight days, without understanding.

Yishmael and family did not stand at Sinai. Yitzchak's did. And we are here today, testifying to the eternal validity of the *Bris*.

What's in a Name?

_____ *Rabbi Bertram Leff*

NAMES HAVE PLAYED AN IMPORTANT ROLE IN JEWISH TRADITION. THE
Midrash (Tanchumah, Haazinu 7) tells us that, לעולם ידבק אדם בשמות
צדיק להיות הראוי לבנו לקרא — "One should always give his son a name
worthy for him to become a righteous person." The name given at
the *Bris* can thus be a contributing factor to our aspirations for the
child.

Three times during the *Bris* ritual we proclaim, יכנס כן לברית שנכנס כשם
טובים ולמעשים ולחפה לתורה — "Just as he has entered into the *Bris,* the
covenant of Abraham, so may he enter into the study and observance of
the Torah, the marriage canopy, and a life of good deeds."

There are many interpretations that can be assigned to these words:
Just as the child's *Bris* is celebrated with joy, so may these other occasions be celebrated with *simcha.* Just as the *Bris* is everlasting, so may
the other significant life events be everlasting. Just as we enter into the
covenant of our father, Avraham, with purity of thought and intent, so
may the commitment to the other occasions be pure and sincere.

In the spirit of the Midrash it is possible to add a new dimension to our
understanding of the words of כשם. The name, שם, that a child is given at
the *Bris* should be a source of inspiration for him as he commits himself
to Torah, to *Chuppah,* to building a Jewish home, and to *mitzvos,* to good
deeds.

A name has the power to define an individual and his potential for
righteous living. שנכנס כשם, is a prayer of parents and grandparents and

_____

*Rabbi Leff is former National Director of Synagogue Services at the Orthodox Union and
editor of "Torah Insights" published by the Orthodox Union.*

the community of Israel that the child's future will reveal the potential that is inherent in the name bestowed upon him at the *Bris*.

As an example of how this thought may be applied let us consider my first grandchild's name, Shmuel Baruch. Both names represent great-grandfathers whose lives exemplified commitment to Torah Judaism. Both were immigrants to America who struggled against all the forces of assimilation that could have undermined their faith. Nevertheless, they triumphed over them and produced a generation of committed Jews, faithful to Torah, *Mitzvos* and the continuity of *Yiddishkeit* on these alien shores. It is our hope that our Shmuel Baruch will continue on the path paved by his great-grandfathers of blessed memory.

Both names, Shmuel and Baruch are names of biblical heroes. Shmuel is the prophet who led the Jewish people as they established the royal Davidic dynasty. Baruch is the faithful disciple of the prophet Jeremiah.

What were the unique characteristics that the biblical Shmuel and Baruch possessed that should be a source of inspiration and an indication of the potential that lies within our new member of the Jewish community?

The very name Shmuel was given to the prophet by his mother, Chana, because, "I asked him from G-d." All of life is a gift from G-d and if our Shmuel will make this principle the guiding light of his life then he will realize that this gift must be nurtured and fashioned into an instrument of service to G-d, Israel, and mankind.

The Talmud (*Shabbos* 56a) describes Shmuel *HaNavi* as the example par excellence of outreach to the Jewish people. "Shmuel the righteous, used to travel to all the places of Israel and judge them in their towns." It is our prayer that our Shmuel will not only be concerned with himself and his immediate surroundings but will reach out to all Jews and bring them closer to the teachings of Sinai.

May G-d bless our Shmuel with the words that describe Shmuel, the prophet, "And the lad Shmuel grew up and וטוב גם עם ה' וגם עם אנשים — "and his relationship with G-d and Man was good."

The only biblical personality whose name is Baruch is Baruch Ben Neriah, the faithful disciple of the prophet, Jeremiah. The Talmud (*Megillah* 17b) teaches us, "For as long as Baruch the son of Neriah was alive his disciple Ezra did not leave him to emigrate to Eretz Yisrael" and help build the Temple of Jerusalem. For, גדול תלמוד תורה יותר מבנין בית

המקדש — "The study of Torah is greater than the building of the *Beis Hamikdash.*"

Ezra's devotion to his teacher, Baruch, was a reward for Baruch's commitment to his teacher, the prophet, Jeremiah. The relationship between a *rebbe* and a *talmid* is a blessing both for the teacher and his student. It is a bond of loyalty to Torah and service to Hashem and His people. May our Baruch find such a relationship of *rebbe* and *talmid* and become a great student and teacher of Torah and thus contribute to the building of the *Beis Hamikdash* in our time.

כשם שנכנס — The name Shmuel Baruch given to him at his *Bris* will hopefully inspire him to reach the potential inherent in his name. It is our prayer that our Shmuel, a gift of G-d, will be Baruch, a blessing to all of us.

A Name's Significance

_____ Rabbi Steven Weil_

W hen hearing the exciting news of the birth of a child, the usual
questions ensue — Was it a boy or girl? How much did he or she
weigh? Does the baby look like Mommy or Daddy? One obvious question
that we don't ask is the baby's name. For Jews, naming a child represents
much more than filling out a birth certificate, and therefore its Jewish
naming coincides with a meaningful religious occasion. A girl is named
at the time of a public Torah reading, and a boy is named at his *Bris Milah.*
Until these ceremonies take place, the child is not called by any name,
and unlike such features as his or her size, appearance and temperament,
the name is not a characterization of the child that the parents will share
with others.

Rabbi Shimon Schwab explained the reason for withholding the
name of the baby from a practical, utilitarian viewpoint. A parent
is overcome by many emotions when naming a child. In a quest to give
their child a name that is befitting and a name that carries a sense
of mission or aspiration, the parents select the name of a loved one who
has passed away or an individual who represented and embodied the
goals they envision for their child and hope he will attain. Because the
new child links the generations and perpetuates the family it is con-
ceivable that there will be many strong opinions as to what the
name should be or who the child should be named after. In order to
avoid possible arguments and hurt feelings at what should be a most
joyous occasion, the child's name is not revealed until it is "official"
and unchangeable. At this point, all that the family and friends can

Rabbi Weil is rav of Beth Jacob Congregation, Beverly Hills, California.

constructively do is rejoice in who the baby is and who he will, G-d willing grow to be.

Rabbi Saul Zuker offers a second explanation which deals with this *halachah* from a more philosophical and conceptual perspective. The reason for the delay in naming a child until his *Bris* is because every Jewish person has a dialectical existence. Firstly, each of us is a unique, distinct individual, possessing our own strengths, weaknesses, and personality. Our *personal* component is referred to as the "*Yachid*" (יחיד) which is characterized by our name. The way we refer to ourselves and who we are is our *communal* personality as a member of the covenental community. We are each an integral part of what is called *Klal Yisrael*. The Jewish people as a whole is a vibrant dynamic entity that truly has a life of its own and is dependent upon each individual member.

By definition, no Jewish person is complete as just a *Yachid* — as only an individual. Being a part of the *Klal* is just as essential in defining who we are. A baby boy first enters the *Klal* at his *Bris Milah,* for at that time he becomes a member of the covenant of Avraham *Avinu.* Prior to that milestone, we do not give him a name, for his personal existence can not begin until his communal existence begins. He simply can not function as a *Yachid* until he becomes part of the covenental community, *Klal Yisrael.* It is only after the actual circumcision takes place that his name is given — ויקרא שמו בישראל — and he can begin the arduous task of growing and developing both human dimensions, as an individual and as a member of the Jewish people.

May the רך הנמול develop as a Torah-true individual and communal personality under the loving guidance of his parents. We wish the parents *berachah* and *hatzlachah* in this vital endeavor and may you and we derive great *nachas* from your son.

Pidyon Haben

Rabbi Simcha Krauss

THE MITZVAH OF PIDYON HABEN IS RELATIVELY EASY TO UNDERSTAND. Originally, as the story of Yaakov and Esav demonstrates, it was the firstborn who were consecrated to perform the _Avodah_ (service) in the _Beis Hamikdash._ The firstborn were also consecrated in Egypt. The very fact that the _Ribbono Shel Olam_ saved the firstborn of _Bnai Yisrael,_ while visiting destruction over the Egyptian firstborn, was a possessive act of G-d demonstrating that the _Bechorim_ belong to Him.

Hence, although the firstborn do not serve in the _Beis Hamikdash_ (a consequence of the golden calf tragedy), still they retain sanctity which has to be redeemed.

What is more difficult to understand is the actual ceremony. The ceremony of _Pidyon Haben_ begins with the father bringing his firstborn son to the _Kohen._ The _Kohen_ then asks the father, "What would you prefer the five _shekalim_ or your child?" The father answers, obviously, that he would rather part with the five _shekalim_ and keep his firstborn son. He then hands the five _shekalim_ to the _Kohen_ and the _Kohen_ "returns" the child to his father.

This ritual seems incomprehensible. When the _Kohen_ asks the father whether he prefers his son or the five _shekalim,_ is there any doubt what the father will choose? And even if, once in a million, a father would sell his son for money, would five _shekalim_ be sufficient?

I believe that the question the _Kohen_ asks the father has a different meaning.

Parents love their children. The love of parent for child is boundless.

Rabbi Krauss is rav of Young Israel of Hillcrest, Flushing, New York.

That love expresses itself in the fact that the parents make certain that the child's *physical* needs are met. It further expresses itself in the parents' constant worries about the child's physical existence.

But this worry that the child be healthy, that he grows and develops has to be expressed also at the *spiritual* level. This is demonstrated by educating him Jewishly and by living in a Jewish environment. The parents must show through their actions that *Mitzvos,* like *shemiras Shabbos, kashrus,* etc. are observed even at the cost of economic hardship. Tuition can be a big financial burden on a family. The cost of kosher food is also more expensive than that of other food. *Shemiras Shabbos* often entails great economic sacrifice.

This is what the *Kohen* asks the father. Do you want your child? Do you want him to continue your lineage and your heritage? Then you should know that at times you will have to part with your money. *Shemiras ha'mitzvos* demands many financial expenditures. By giving the five *shekalim* you show me, albeit symbolically, that you are ready to sacrifice for your son's spiritual development. Now, I am certain that the child will remain yours forever.

We find a comparable idea in *Tanach. Shmuel I* begins with the story of Chana and Elkanah, a childless couple, entreating G-d to help them. Chana prays and, indeed, she is blessed with a son, Shmuel. When Shmuel is weaned and Chana comes to the Tabernacle in Shilo to offer thanks for this gift of motherhood she says: "For this child I did pray, and G-d granted me my request, which I asked of Him. I also have lent him to G-d; all the days that he lives, he is loaned (dedicated) to G-d" (*Shmuel I* 1:27-28).

Chana's words seem, prima facie, incomprehensible. She begins by saying, "For this child I did pray" and then she continues that since G-d granted her wish she is therefore sending this child away. If Chana so anxiously prayed for a child, why, all of a sudden, is she sending him away?

Rav Yosef Dov Soloveitchik, *zt"l,* the Rav, gave a wonderful answer. At times, he said, we gain something and it remains ours, precisely because we give it away. For example, a Jew lives in Wichita, Kansas, far removed from the center of Jewish learning. If the Jew wants his child to be a *ben Torah* he must send him away to a Yeshiva. Keeping the child near him in Wichita is almost a guarantee of losing him. Paradoxically, by sending him away, the parents will have done something positive to keep their child.

This is an extreme example. But we all know that at times, by giving something away, one keeps it. In the *Pidyon Haben* ritual this is demonstrated with the use of money. Indeed, the *Kohen* asks the new father, do you want to keep this son, do you want to make certain that your son will continue your ideals and your heritage? Then, you have to know that it will cost you. The father, of course, realizes what the stakes are and, since ישראל כשרים הם answers, that indeed I want my son and I will do everything possible to ensure that this newborn will be another link in the eternal chain of *Knesses Yisrael.*

The Upsharing & The Wimple Rituals
Two Customs with a Common Root

_____ _Rabbi Ephraim H. Sturm_

A WOMAN WHO HAD JUST GIVEN BIRTH ASKED A RENOWNED _TZADDIK_ WHEN SHE should begin to teach her child to be a Torah scholar and a deeply observant Jew. The Rebbe answered that she was already more than nine months late. This apocryphal story has educational and mystical implications. However, Jewish communities have accepted, as a rule of thumb, that one should begin teaching a child after the third birthday.

Communities differ regarding the ritual for this right of passage. Observant German Jewry developed the Wimple procedure, while other communities perform the act of _Upsharing._ Both of these rituals and even those observant Jews who simply introduce the child to the _Aleph Bais_ on the third birthday and do not practice either _Upsharing_ or the Wimple, base the three year time frame on a _Midrash Tanchumah_ which concludes that the beginning of a life-long learning process at the age of three is related to the planting of a tree.

Our Torah teaches us that a tree's fruit of the first three years is forbidden under the laws of _Orlah_ — freely translated as "closed." The fruit of the fourth year is sacred and therefore must be consumed only in Jerusalem.

Based on the verse, "for man is a tree of the field" (_Devarim_ 20:19), the Midrash mystically equates the child to a tree. This relationship, in practice, notes that for the first three years a child is like _Orlah,_ or not "open" to education. On the fourth year, the father is mandated to sanctify the

Rabbi Sturm is a chaplain at Roosevelt Hospital, New York City, and Emeritus Executive Vice President of the Young Israel. He is a lecturer at the New York College of Podiatric Medicine and a Lieutenant Colonel in the New York Guard (ret.).

child, similar to the fruit that is sanctified then, through the performance of a single *mitzvah*.

The *Ramah* suggests that the child should be taught to recognize Hebrew letters, so that he may learn to read. Other suggests that teaching a child is based subjectively upon the readiness of the child to comprehend. However, there seems to be a consensus that at his third birthday the child should be adorned with a *tallis katan* and a *yarmulke*.

The Upsharing

THE *UPSHARING* CEREMONY WHICH ENTAILS GIVING THE MALE CHILD HIS FIRST haircut at, or soon after, his third birthday is followed by a joyous *seudah* or a religious festive meal. As noted, this custom is based on an earlier custom of not training the child in the observance of *mitzvos* until the third birthday, which in turn is based upon the *Midrash Tanchumah* wherein an analogy is made between a child and a young tree.

Though classic Yiddish is a beautiful and almost poetic language, replete with Biblical, Talmudic and local colloquialisms, the employment of the Yiddish word *"Upsharing"* as related to the child's first haircut, does not do justice to the deep meaning of the ritual — in fact it may be misleading.

It is said that a sculptor, through his mind's eye, sees the finished form in the slab of marble. The hammer and chisel then are employed merely to cut away all the excess material surrounding the conceived form within. Cutting the child's hair may be necessary, not for its own sake but in order to reveal, for the first time, the child's *payos*. The ultimate purpose of the haircut then is not shortening the hair but the revelation of the *mitzvah* of לא תקפו פאת ראשכם — "You shall not round off the edge of your scalp" (*Vayikra* 19:27). Unlike the sculptor who disregards the chips, the Jewish people utilize even the discarded hair as a vehicle for performing *mitzvos*, hence the custom of donating golden coins amounting to the weight of the hair.

At the *Upsharing seudah*, some even suggest that the father, who now introduced the child to the majestic world of Torah and *Mitzvos* — through the *tallis katan* and the *kipah* which are external and the *payos* which are part of the very being of the child — should recite the blessing of המקום יאיר את עיניך בתורתו — "May the Almighty illuminate your eyes through the study of His Torah."

An extension of the *Upsharing* ritual suggests that because it is rooted in sanctity, the actual haircut which will reveal the *payos* should be done by a prestigious Jew. Perhaps it is also the origin of the Israeli custom of performing this act at the grave of Rabbi Shimon Ben Yochai, or at the grave of another *tzaddik*.

Once we establish a definite objective date for the *Upsharing* — the third birthday — ancillary questions will arise about the permissibility of *Upsharing* on Friday, if the birthday should occur on Shabbos, or the permissibility of *Upsharing* on *Chol Hamoed*. The *Levush Mordechai*, and the *minhag* of Chabad adhere to the technical third birthday, and, therefore, do not permit an earlier act, even l'*Kavod Shabbos* or *Chol Hamoed*. The *minhag* of Belz and Popov do allow an earlier haircutting. Obviously other questions will arise concerning *Sefirah*.

Having noted all this it is still incumbent upon us to indicate that the *Sefer Shulchan Aruch Gavoha* (*siman* תקל״א) states that the *Upsharing* ceremony should be done at the age of five. The *Sefer Chinuch Yisrael* suggests that the ritual be performed when the child reaches his second birthday.

The Wimple

T O PROTECT THE NEWLY CIRCUMCISED CHILD FROM IRRITATION OR INFECTION the wound is bandaged with a rather long piece of material. After a few days when the bandages are no longer needed, some German Ashkenazic Jews have the bandages — which are then referred to as Wimple — embroidered, embossed, or artistically painted with the name of the child, some reference to his ancestors and his birthday. On the child's third birthday, or close to it, when the child no longer needs diapers, the father takes the child to the synagogue for the first time. On this occasion it is customary to present the Wimple to the synagogue to bind the *Sefer Torah* before covering it with a *Mantle*. The synagogue will then either continue to use it as a binding for the *Sefer Torah*, or keep it in its archives. Usually, the third birthday is considered the ideal time for the child to be introduced to the synagogue.

The custom of utilizing the Wimple as a binding for the *Sefer Torah* is first found in the *Sefer* of the *Maharil*, in which it is related that the *Maharil Segal* was a *Sandak* at a *Bris* where it was discovered that there was no material with which to bind the circumcision wound. The *Maharil Segal* said that one should use the material which was used to bind the *Sefer Torah,* obviously basing his decision on the law of *sakanos nefashos.* He ruled that the sanctity of the Torah binding is not diminished by using it to protect the child. In passing, it is also noted that he advocated that the father donate a token gift to the synagogue to avoid the problem of having a personal gain through the use of a religious object (להנות מן ההקדש בחנם).

This incident and subsequent *halachic* rulings, as dramatic as they may be, do not explain the theological background and how it relates to the Wimple custom.

The author of *Minhagei Yisrael* writes that Rabbi Yehoshyua Noibrit advised him that the custom of presenting a Wimple to the Synagogue on the child's third birthday is based upon the *halachic* rule of *Orlah* (as explained above). He also notes that this ritual and the *Upsharing* ritual, is accompanied with the child's first introduction to the *Aleph Bais.*

THE *UPSHARING* AND THE WIMPLE RITUAL ON THE CHILD'S THIRD BIRTHDAY, AT which time he is given his first lesson in the *Aleph Bais,* as well as those who introduce the child to Torah without either of these rituals have the common root of "for man is like the tree of the field" and all subsequent relationships to the laws of *Orlah.*

It is safe to propose that the *Upsharing* reflects the three-year *objective* time frame and the Wimple reflects the *subjective* child oriented method. Both of these rituals, in turn, are based upon the relationship of a young sapling to a young child, as noted in the Midrash.

This comparison leads scholars to suggest that just as a tree needs seeds, water and weeding, so too, the child's soul represents the seed which is to be developed through the waters of Torah. To maximize the development of a child one must weed out harmful social influences. Furthermore, just as young saplings need the protection of two braces in order to grow straight, so too, the child needs the strong support of his parents.

Is a Woman Permitted to Perform a Bris Milah?

_____ *Debbie Schwartz and Elizabeth Muschel*

IN *SEFER SHEMOS,* THE TORAH TELLS US OF THE ONLY OCCURRENCE WHEN A mother performed her son's *Bris Milah:* — "So Tzipporah took a sharp stone and cut off the foreskin of her son and touched it to his feet; and she said, "You caused my bridegroom's bloodshed!" So he released him; then she said, "A bridegroom's bloodshed was because of circumcision" (*Shemos* 4:25-26).

What were the circumstances that caused Tzipporah to take up the knife and perform the circumcision of her son? G-d had commanded Moshe to return to Egypt. Moshe realized that although he needed to circumcise his son, Eliezer, he could not do so before leaving for Egypt. He knew that his son would be in danger if he traveled within three days of the *Bris.* Moshe struggled with the conflict of potentially disobeying G-d's orders to go to Egypt immediately, versus performing Eliezer's *Bris* on time. *Rashi* explains, that Moshe's sin was that upon arrival at the inn on the way to Egypt, he did not *immediately* address the issue of his son's *Bris.* Rather, he went to make lodging arrangements. This delay is what caused the angel to seek his death. *Rashi* explains that the angel who came to kill Moshe assumed the form of a snake and began to swallow Moshe up until the point of his loins. Tzipporah, upon seeing that Moshe's life was in danger, and perceiving the reason for it, immediately began to perform the *Milah.*

Debbie Schwartz has a Master of Science degree in psychology and serves on the boards of the Yeshiva University High School and Shaare Zedek Hospital.
Elizabeth Muschel, a freelance writer, lives in Monsey, New York with her husband and four sons.

However, according to other interpretations (ציץ אליעזר) Moshe was exempt from performing the *Bris* because he was engrossed in the *mitzvah* of *Yetzias Mitzrayim,* and was therefore not in danger, rather the baby was the one in danger. Combining both of the above interpretations, we can conclude that Tzipporah's act was motivated by both a wifely **and** maternal instinct — an act done swiftly and decisively in order to save her husband's life and her child's life. She quickly took a knife, and without a second thought, circumcised her baby, and threw the foreskin at Moshe's feet, thus saving his life.

Was Tzipporah in fact, as a woman, permitted to perform the *Bris Milah?* Rav Yosef Caro says, הכל כשרין למול ואפילו עבד ואפילו אשה, ואפילו קטן — "Everyone is kosher to do a *Bris,* even a slave, a woman or a child" (*Shulchan Aruch Yoreh Deiah* רס"ד). There is a *machlokes* cited in *Avodah Zarah* 27 between Rav and Rabbi Yochanan as to whether a woman is indeed permitted to perform the *Bris.* Rav says, she may not perform a *Bris,* because she has never had a *Bris* done to herself. Rav Yochanan says a woman can perform a *Bris,* because a woman is born as though she is already circumcised. The Gemora in explaining Rav goes on to say that Tzipporah may have appointed someone else to perform the *Bris* for her. Since she initiated it, the Torah gives her the credit. Another interpretation says that Tzipporah began the *Bris* and Moshe completed it. The *Ramah,* in *Shulchan Aruch paskins* like *Tosfos* that a woman should not perform a *Bris.*

Notwithstanding the *halachah,* there have been several instances throughout Jewish history of women performing *Bris Milah* on their own sons. These poignant stories all display tremendous *mesiras nefesh,* a heartful sacrifice on the part of Jewish mothers. During the Roman Empire, circumcision was forbidden, and had to be performed in utmost secrecy. Rabbi Yehudah *HaNasi's* mother, at great personal risk, made sure that her baby had a *Bris Milah.* The circumcision was reported to the Roman authorities. The mother and child were taken into custody, and were jailed in Rome awaiting trial. A Roman noblewoman, hearing the compelling story, came to visit the young mother in jail. The noblewoman was overwhelmed with the bravery of R' Yehudah's mother. She offered to switch her own son with the Jewish baby in order to foil the Romans. R' Yehudah's mother agreed, and the switch was made. When the baby was revealed to be uncircumcised, both mother and baby were freed.

The young baby that was nursed and cared for by R' Yehudah's mother during her time in jail grew up to be the Roman emperor, Antonius. Antonius proved to be a great friend and sympathizer to the Jewish people.

Similarly, Rabbi Israel Spira relates the story of a Jewish mother's bravery during the Holocaust, as reported by Dr. Yaffa Eliach, in her book *Chassidic Tales of the Holocaust.* He tells of a Jewish woman heading to her death and demanding a knife from the Nazi guard. The Nazi is so taken aback by her forcefulness, that he hands her the knife, assuming that she would use it to commit suicide. Instead, she bent down and swiftly picked up a bundle of rags and with a steady hand, used the knife while reciting the following blessing: "Blessed are You, Hashem our G-d, King of the Universe, who has sanctified us with His commandments, and has commanded us to perform the circumcision." The cry of a baby was heard, and the onlookers realized that she had just performed a *Bris Milah* on her own son. She then looked up to the sky and said, "G-d of the Universe, you have given me a healthy child. I am returning to you a wholesome, Kosher Jew." She then returned the blood-stained knife to the Nazi, along with her son.

As noted above, women may not perform a *Bris Milah,* according to *Halachah,* unless a man is not available. However, the Jewish historical experience provides evidence that through the ages, Jewish mothers have been full participants in the circumcisions of their sons. Perhaps there is a lesson here. The next time we witness this beautiful ceremony reenacted — a Jewish infant boy entering the Covenant of Abraham — it would serve us well to remember the sacrifices and *mesiras nefesh* endured by every Jewish mother throughout history in bringing their sons to this day.